a Passion for Cables

Weaving and waving through this stunning knit collection is a tremendous variety of easy cable patterns. Show off your curves in a red cabled dress. Put a twist on your fashion focus by knitting a fresh blue halter dress. This ultra-chic cabled clothing includes a tunic, a skirt, and a split-neck shell, as well as a half-dozen sweaters and tops. A total of 14 designs await your discovery. Choose your favorite yarn, pick up your knitting needles, and add a world of texture to your wardrobe!

LEISURE ARTS, INC.
Little Rock, Arkansas

EDITORIAL STAFF

Vice President and Editor-in-Chief
Sandra Graham Case
Executive Publications Director
Cheryl Nodine Gunnells
Senior Publications Director
Susan White Sullivan
Designer Relations Director
Debra Nettles
Knit and Crochet Publications Director
Mary Sullivan Hutcheson
Prepress Director
Mark Hawkins
Art Publications Director
Rhonda Shelby
Technical Writer
Linda Luder
Contributing Editor
Valesha M. Kirksey
Editorial Writer
Susan McManus Johnson
Art Category Manager
Chaska Lucas
Imaging Technician
Mark R. Potter
Photography Manager
Katherine Atchison
Contributing Photography Stylist
Angela Alexander
Contributing Photographer
Jason Masters
Publishing Systems Administrator
Becky Riddle
Publishing Systems Assistants
Clint Hanson and John Rose

BUSINESS STAFF

Chief Operating Officer
Tom Siebenmorgen
Vice President, Sales and Marketing
Pam Stebbins
Director of Sales and Services
Margaret Reinold
Vice President, Operations
Jim Dittrich
Comptroller, Operations
Rob Thieme
Retail Customer Service Manager
Stan Raynor
Print Production Manager
Fred F. Pruss

Made in the United States of America.
ISBN 1-57486-505-6
Library of Congress Control Number: 2006939434
10 9 8 7 6 5 4 3 2 1

Column Dress

Column Dress

Shown on pages 4 and 5.

⬤⬛⬛◻ INTERMEDIATE

Size	Finished Chest Measurement
X-Small	32" (81.5 cm)
Small	36" (91.5 cm)
Medium	40" (101.5 cm)
Large	44" (112 cm)

Size Note: Instructions are written for size X-Small with sizes Small, Medium, and Large in braces { }. Instructions will be easier to read if you circle all the numbers pertaining to your size. If only one number is given, it applies to all sizes.

MATERIALS

Medium Weight Yarn
[1¹/₂ ounces, 84 yards
(40 grams, 77 meters) per ball]:
    16{18-20-22} balls
Straight knitting needles, size 8 (5 mm)
    or size needed for gauge
Cable needle
Yarn needle

GAUGE: In pattern (slightly stretched),
    24 sts = 4" (10 cm) and
    16 rows = 2³/₈" (6 cm)
    In Stockinette Stitch,
    17 sts and 25 rows = 4" (10 cm)

STITCH GUIDE

CABLE 6 FRONT *(abbreviated C6F)*
 (uses next 6 sts)
Slip next 4 sts onto cable needle and hold at **front** of work, K2 from left needle, slip last 2 sts from cable needle **back** to left needle and purl them, then K2 from cable needle.

BODY (Make 2)

Cast on 98{110-122-134} sts.

Row 1: P2, (K2, P2) across.

Row 2 (Right side): K2, (P2, K2) across.

Rows 3-7: Repeat Rows 1 and 2 twice, then repeat Row 1 once **more**.

Row 8: K2, (P2, C6F, P2, K2) across.

Repeat Rows 1-8 for pattern until Body measures approximately 36¼{37½-37½-38½}"/ 92{95-95-98} cm from cast on edge **or 2" (5 cm) less than desired length to shoulder**, ending by working Row 7.

SHAPING

Row 1: K2, ★ P2 tog *(Fig. 4, page 92)*, slip next 4 sts onto cable needle and hold in **front** of work, K2 from left needle, slip last 2 sts from cable needle **back** to left needle and purl them together, K2 from cable needle, P2 tog, K2; repeat from ★ across: 74{83-92-101} sts.

Row 2: P2, (K1, P2) across.

Row 3: K2, (P1, K2) across.

Rows 4-8: Repeat Rows 2 and 3 twice, then repeat Row 2 once **more**.

Row 9: K2, ★ P1, slip next 3 sts onto cable needle and hold in **front** of work, K2 from left needle, slip last st from cable needle **back** to left needle and purl it, K2 from cable needle, P1, K2; repeat from ★ across.

Rows 10-14: Repeat Rows 2 and 3 twice, then repeat Row 2 once **more**.

Bind off all sts in **knit**.

FINISHING

Sew each shoulder seam leaving a(n) 8¼{8¾-9¼-9¾}"/21-{22-23.5-25} cm neck opening.

Sew each side seam leaving an 7{7½-8-8½}"/ 18{19-20.5-21.5} cm armhole opening.

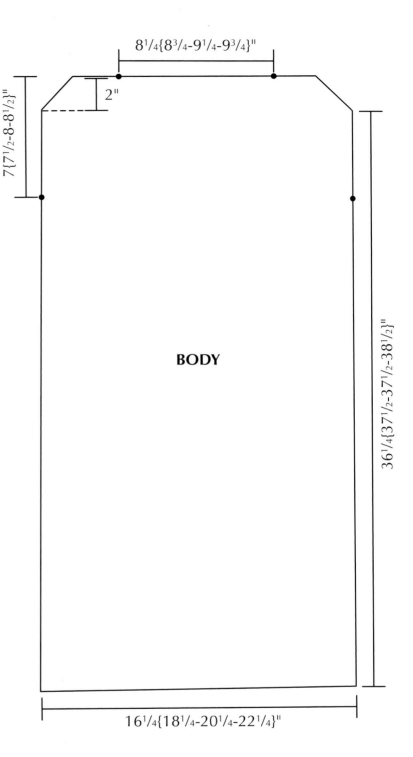

8¼{8¾-9¼-9¾}"

2"

7{7½-8-8½}"

BODY

36¼{37½-37½-38½}"

16¼{18¼-20¼-22¼}"

Note: Dress includes two edge stitches.

Halter Dress

Halter Dress

Shown on pages 8 and 9.

◼◼◼◻ INTERMEDIATE

Size	Finished Chest Measurement
X-Small	28½" (72.5 cm)
Small	33" (84 cm)
Medium	37¾" (94 cm)
Large	42¼" (107.5 cm)

Size Note: Instructions are written for size X-Small with sizes Small, Medium and Large in braces { }. Instructions will be easier to read if you circle all the numbers pertaining to your size. If only one number is given, it applies to all sizes.

MATERIALS

Bulky Weight Yarn **BULKY 5**
[5 ounces, 153 yards
(140 grams, 140 meters) per skein]:
    5{5-6-7} skeins
Straight knitting needles, size 13 (9 mm) **or**
    size needed for gauge
29" (73.5 cm) Circular knitting needle,
    size 13 (9 mm) **or** size needed for gauge
Cable needle
Stitch holder
Markers
Crochet hook, size J (6 mm)

GAUGE: In pattern (slightly stretched),
    14 sts = 4" (10 cm);
    18 rows/rnds = 5½" (14 cm)

STITCH GUIDE

CABLE 6 BACK *(abbreviated C6B)*
(uses next 6 sts)
Slip next 4 sts onto cable needle and hold at **back** of work, K2 from left needle, slip last 2 sts from cable needle **back** to left needle and purl them, then K2 from cable needle.

CABLE 6 FRONT *(abbreviated C6F)*
(uses next 6 sts)
Slip next 4 sts onto cable needle and hold at **front** of work, K2 from left needle, slip last 2 sts from cable needle **back** to left needle and purl them, then K2 from cable needle.

CABLE 5 BACK *(abbreviated C5B)*
(uses next 5 sts)
Slip next 3 sts onto cable needle and hold at **back** of work, K2 from left needle, slip last st from cable needle **back** to left needle and purl it, then K2 from cable needle.

CABLE 3 FRONT *(abbreviated C3F)*
(uses next 3 sts)
Slip next 2 sts onto cable needle and hold at **front** of work, K1 from left needle, slip last st from cable needle **back** to left needle and purl it, then K1 from cable needle.

BODY

FRONT

With straight knitting needles, cast on 50{58-66-74} sts.

Row 1: K2, (P2, K2) across.

Row 2 (Right side)**:** P2, (K2, P2) across.

Rows 3-5: Repeat Rows 1 and 2 once, then repeat Row 1 once **more**.

Row 6: P2, (C6B, P2) across.

Row 7: K2, (P2, K2) across.

Row 8: P2, (K2, P2) across.

Row 9: K2, (P2, K2) across.

Row 10: P2, K2, P2, (C6F, P2) across to last 4 sts, K2, P2.

Row 11: K2, (P2, K2) across.

Row 12: P2, (K2, P2) across.

Row 13: K2, (P2, K2) across.

Row 14: P2, (C6B, P2) across.

Row 15: K2, (P2, K2) across.

Row 16: P2, (K2, P2) across.

Row 17: K2, (P2, K2) across; cut yarn and leave sts on straight knitting needle until the Joining Rnd.

BACK

With circular knitting needle, cast on 50{58-66-74} sts.

Rows 1-17: Work same as Front; at end of Row 17, do **not** cut yarn and leave sts on circular knitting needle.

Begin working Body in one piece to underarm.

Joining Rnd (Right side)**:** Continuing to work Back on circular knitting needle, † P2, K2, P2, (C6F, P2) across to last 4 sts, K2, P2 †, place a marker to mark side **(see Markers, page 92)**; working Front sts off of straight knitting needle, repeat from † to † once, place a marker to mark the beginning of the rnd **(see Knitting in the Round, page 91)**: 100{116-132-148} sts.

Rnds 1-3: P2, (K2, P2) across to side marker, slip marker, P2, (K2, P2) around.

Rnd 4: P2, (C6B, P2) across to side marker, slip marker, P2, (C6B, P2) around.

Rnds 5-7: P2, (K2, P2) across to side marker, slip marker, P2, (K2, P2) around.

Rnd 8: P2, K2, P2, (C6F, P2) across to within 4 sts of side marker, K2, P2, slip marker, P2, K2, P2, (C6F, P2) around to last 4 sts, K2, P2.

Repeat Rnds 1-8 for pattern until Body measures approximately 28" (71 cm) from cast on edge **or desired length to underarm**, ending by working Rnd 7.

Next Rnd: Bind off first 50{58-66-74} sts removing side marker (Back), P1, K2, P2, (C6F, P2) across to last 4 sts, K2, P2: 50{58-66-74} sts.

FRONT SHAPING

Row 1: K2, (P2, K2) across.

Row 2: P2, (K2, P2) across.

Row 3: K2, (P2, K2) across.

Row 4 (Right side)**:** P2, (C6B, P2) across.

Row 5: K2, (P2, K2) across.

Row 6: P2, (K2, P2) across.

Instructions continued on page 13.

Row 7: K2, (P2, K2) across.

Row 8: P2, K2, P2, (C6F, P2) across to last 4 sts, K2, P2.

Row 9: K2, (P2, K2) across.

Row 10: P2, (K2, P2) across.

Row 11: K2, ★ P2, K2 tog *(Fig. 3, page 92)*, P2, K2; repeat from ★ across: 44{51-58-65} sts.

Row 12: P2, C5B, ★ P2 tog *(Fig. 4, page 92)*, C5B; repeat from ★ across to last 2 sts, P2: 39{45-51-57} sts.

Row 13: K2, P2, (K1, P2) across to last 2 sts, K2.

Row 14: P2, K2 tog, (P1, K2 tog) across to last 2 sts, P2: 27{31-35-39} sts.

Row 15: K2, P1, (K1, P1) across to last 2 sts, K2.

Row 16: P2, K1, P1, (C3F, P1) across to last 3 sts, K1, P2.

Row 17: K2 tog, P1, (K1, P1) across to last 2 sts, K2 tog: 25{29-33-37} sts.

Row 18: P1, ★ K3 tog *(Fig. 7, page 93)*, P1; repeat from ★ across: 13{15-17-19} sts.

Leave remaining sts on the knitting needle.

FINISHING
See Crochet Stitches, page 94.

Eyelet Row: With **wrong** side facing and using a crochet hook, insert hook in first st on knitting needle, YO and pull up a loop, ch 1 *(Fig. A)*, sc in same st, slide st off knitting needle *(Fig. B)*, sc in each st across sliding st off knitting needle as it is worked; finish off.

Tie: Chain a 60" (152.5) cm length; finish off. Weave through sts on Eyelet Row.

Fig. A　　**Fig. B**

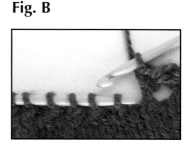

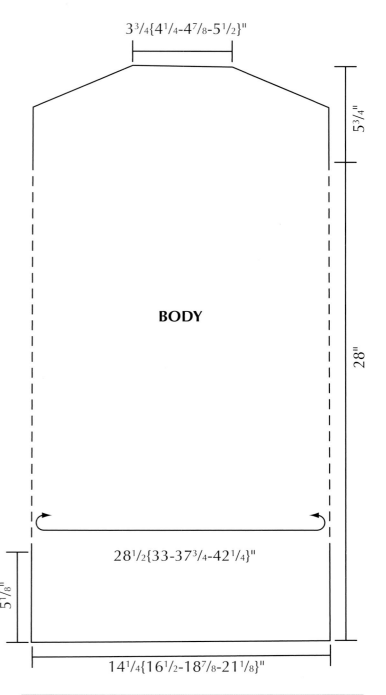

$3^3/_4\{4^1/_4-4^7/_8-5^1/_2\}$"

$5^3/_4$"

28"

BODY

$28^1/_2\{33-37^3/_4-42^1/_4\}$"

$5^1/_8$"

$14^1/_4\{16^1/_2-18^7/_8-21^1/_8\}$"

Note: Dashed lines indicate continuous rounds.

13

Mock Turtleneck

Mock Turtleneck

Shown on pages 14 and 15.

◖◗◗◗◻ **INTERMEDIATE**

Size	Finished Chest Measurement
X-Small	30" (76 cm)
Small	33³/₄" (85.5 cm)
Medium	37¹/₂" (95.5 cm)
Large	41¹/₄" (105 cm)

Size Note: Instructions are written for size X-Small with sizes Small, Medium and Large in braces { }. Instructions will be easier to read if you circle all the numbers pertaining to your size. If only one number is given, it applies to all sizes.

MATERIALS

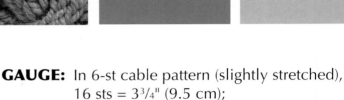

Bulky Weight Yarn
[3 ounces, 135 yards,
(85 grams, 123 meters) per skein]:
   5{5-6-7} skeins
29" (73.5 cm) Circular knitting needle,
   size 11 (8 mm) **or** size needed for gauge
Straight knitting needles, size 11 (8 mm)
Double-pointed knitting needles, size 11 (8 mm)
Cable needle
Stitch holders - 6
Markers
Crochet hook, size J (6 mm)

GAUGE: In 6-st cable pattern (slightly stretched),
   16 sts = 3³/₄" (9.5 cm);
   16 rows/rnds = 4¹/₄" (10.75 cm)

STITCH GUIDE

CABLE 6 FRONT *(abbreviated C6F)*
   (uses next 6 sts)
Slip next 4 sts onto cable needle and hold at **front** of work, K2 from left needle, slip last 2 sts from cable needle **back** to left needle and purl them, then K2 from cable needle.

CABLE 6 BACK *(abbreviated C6B)*
   (uses next 6 sts)
Slip next 4 sts onto cable needle and hold at **back** of work, K2 from left needle, slip last 2 sts from cable needle **back** to left needle and purl them, then K2 from cable needle.

CABLE 5 FRONT *(abbreviated C5F)*
   (uses next 5 sts)
Slip next 3 sts onto cable needle and hold at **front** of work, K2 from left needle, slip last st from cable needle **back** to left needle and purl it, then K2 from cable needle.

CABLE 5 BACK *(abbreviated C5B)*
   (uses next 5 sts)
Slip next 3 sts onto cable needle and hold at **back** of work, K2 from left needle, slip last st from cable needle **back** to left needle and purl it, then K2 from cable needle.

Body is worked in one piece to underarm.

BODY

With circular knitting needle, cast on 128{144-160-176} sts; place a marker to mark the beginning of the rnd *(see Knitting in the Round and Markers, pages 91 and 92)*.

Rnds 1-5: (K2, P2) around.

Rnd 6 (Right side)**:** (C6F, P2) around.

Rnds 7 and 8: (K2, P2) around.

Rnd 9: (K2, P2) around to last 4 sts, slip last 4 sts and the marker onto cable needle and hold in **back** of work *(the marker will fall off the cable needle but it should be placed after the 2 purl sts have been worked and not at the beginning of the first cable on the next rnd)*.

Rnd 10: (C6B, P2) around.

Rnds 11-13: (K2, P2) around.

Repeat Rnds 6-13 for pattern until Body measures approximately 15¹/₂" (39.5 cm) from cast on edge **or desired length to underarm**, ending by working Rnd 12.

Next Rnd: K2, (P2, K2) around to last 2 sts, P1, move the beginning of the rnd marker before the last st.

FRONT

Row 1 (Right side)**:** With straight knitting needles, P1, C6F, (P2, C6F) 7{8-9-10} times, P1, leave remaining sts unworked on circular knitting needle (Back): 64{72-80-88} sts.

Row 2: K1, P2, (K2, P2) across to last st, K1.

Row 3: P1, K2, (P2, K2) across to last st, P1.

Row 4: K1, P2, K2, P2, K2 tog *(Fig. 3, page 92)*, P2, (K2, P2) across to last 9 sts, K2 tog, P2, K2, P2, K1: 62{70-78-86} sts.

Row 5: P1, K2, P2 tog *(Fig. 4, page 92)*, C5B, P2, (C6B, P2) 5{6-7-8} times, C5B, P2 tog, K2, P1: 60{68-76-84} sts.

Row 6: (K1, P2) 3 times, K2 tog, P2, (K2, P2) 9{11-13-15} times, K2 tog, (P2, K1) 3 times: 58{66-74-82} sts.

Row 7: (P1, K2) 4 times, (P2, K2) 9{11-13-15} times, P1, (K2, P1) 3 times.

Row 8: (K1, P2) 4 times, K2 tog, P2, (K2, P2) 7{9-11-13} times, K2 tog, (P2, K1) 4 times: 56{64-72-80} sts.

Row 9: P1, (C5F, P1) twice, C6F, (P2, C6F) 3{4-5-6} times, P1, (C5F, P1) twice.

Row 10: (K1, P2) 5 times, K2 tog, P2, (K2, P2) 5{7-9-11} times, K2 tog, (P2, K1) 5 times: 54{62-70-78} sts.

Row 11: (P1, K2) 6 times, (P2, K2) 5{7-9-11} times, P1, (K2, P1) 5 times.

Row 12: (K1, P2) 6 times, K2 tog, (P2, K2 tog) 4{6-8-10} times, (P2, K1) 6 times: 49{55-61-67} sts.

Row 13: P1, K2, P1, (C5B, P1) across to last 3 sts, K2, P1.

Row 14: K1, (P2, K1) across.

Row 15: P1, (K2, P1) across.

Row 16: K1, (P2, K1) across.

Row 17: P1, (C5F, P1) across.

Row 18: K1, (P2, K1) across.

Row 19: P1, (K2, P1) across.

Row 20: K1, (P2, K1) across.

Instructions continued on page 19.

Repeat Rows 13-20 for pattern until Front measures approximately 7{7$\frac{1}{2}$-8-8$\frac{1}{2}$}"/18{19-20.5-21.5} cm, ending by working a **right** side row.

Last Row: Maintaining established pattern, work across first 10{10-13-13} sts, slip sts just worked onto a st holder (right shoulder); work across next 29{35-35-41} sts, slip sts just worked onto a second st holder (neck); work across last 10{10-13-13} sts, slip sts just worked onto a third st holder (left shoulder).

BACK
Row 1: With **right** side facing, using straight knitting needles, and working across sts on circular knitting needle, P1, C6F, (P2, C6F) across to last st, P1: 64{72-80-88} sts.

Beginning with Row 2, complete same as Front.

Slip sts from Front and Back right shoulder st holders onto double-pointed knitting needles. Work 3-Needle Bind off **(Fig. 8, page 93)**.

Repeat for left shoulder.

FINISHING
MOCK TURTLENECK
Rnd 1: With **right** side facing and using double-pointed knitting needles, pick up one st in either shoulder seam at neck edge **(Figs. 9a & b, page 93)**; slip sts from first neck st holder onto empty knitting needle and work across in established pattern, pick up one st in next shoulder seam, slip sts from second neck st holder onto empty knitting needle and work across in established pattern, place a marker to mark the beginning of the rnd: 60{72-72-84} sts.

Work in established pattern around until Mock Turtleneck measures approximately 3" (7.5 cm).

Bind off all sts **loosely.**

ARMHOLE EDGING
See Crochet Stitches, page 94.

Rnd 1: With **right** side facing and using a crochet hook, join yarn with sc at underarm **(see Joining With Sc, page 94)**; sc evenly around armhole edge; join with slip st to first sc.

Rnd 2: Ch 1, sc in Back Loop Only **(Fig. 16, page 94)** of same st and each sc around; join with slip st to **both** loops of first sc, finish off.

Repeat around second Armhole.

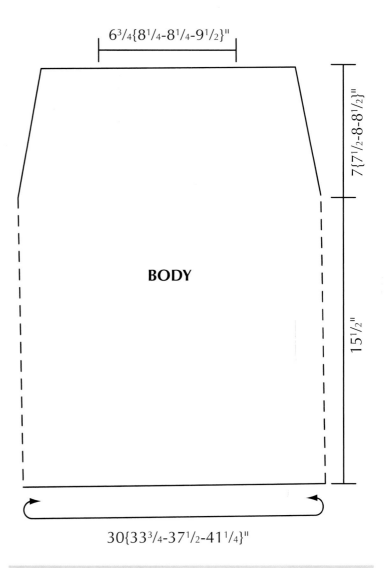

6$\frac{3}{4}$\{8$\frac{1}{4}$-8$\frac{1}{4}$-9$\frac{1}{2}$\}"

7\{7$\frac{1}{2}$-8-8$\frac{1}{2}$\}"

BODY

15$\frac{1}{2}$"

30\{33$\frac{3}{4}$-37$\frac{1}{2}$-41$\frac{1}{4}$\}"

Note: Dashed lines indicate continuous rounds.

19

Turtleneck Sweater

Turtleneck Sweater

Shown on pages 20 and 21.

◖▮▮▯ **INTERMEDIATE**

Size	Finished Chest Measurement
X-Small	26¹/₂" (67.5 cm)
Small	33¹/₄" (84.5 cm)
Medium	36¹/₂" (92.5 cm)
Large	43¹/₄" (110 cm)

Size Note: Instructions are written for size X-Small with sizes Small, Medium and Large in braces { }. Instructions will be easier to read if you circle all the numbers pertaining to your size. If only one number is given, it applies to all sizes.

MATERIALS

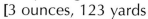

Bulky Weight Yarn
[3 ounces, 123 yards
(85 grams, 113 meters) per skein]:
   8{10-11-12} skeins
Straight knitting needles, size 10 (6 mm) **or**
   size needed for gauge
Double-pointed knitting needles, size 10 (6 mm)
Cable needle
Stitch holders - 2
Marker
Yarn needle

GAUGE: In pattern (slightly stretched),
18 sts = 3³/₄" (9.5 cm) and
16 rows/rnds = 3¹/₄" (8.25 cm)
In Stockinette Stitch,
14 sts and 18 rows/rnds = 4" (10 cm)

STITCH GUIDE

CABLE 6 FRONT (*abbreviated C6F*)
(uses next 6 sts)
Slip next 4 sts onto cable needle and hold at
front of work, K2 from left needle, slip last 2 sts
from cable needle **back** to left needle and purl
them, then K2 from cable needle.

CABLE 6 BACK (*abbreviated C6B*)
(uses next 6 sts)
Slip next 4 sts onto cable needle and hold at
back of work, K2 from left needle, slip last 2 sts
from cable needle **back** to left needle and purl
them, then K2 from cable needle.

BODY (Make 2)

With straight knitting needles, cast on
66{82-90-106} sts.

Row 1: K2, (P2, K2) across.

Row 2 (Right side): P2, (K2, P2) across.

Rows 3-11: Repeat Rows 1 and 2, 4 times; then
repeat Row 1 once **more**.

Row 12: P2, (K2, P2) 1{0-1-0} time(s) *(see Zeros, page 92)*, C6F, P2, (K2, P2, C6F, P2) across to last 4{0-4-0} sts, (K2, P2) 1{0-1-0} time(s).

Row 13: K2, (P2, K2) across.

Row 14: P2, (K2, P2) across.

Rows 15-19: Repeat Rows 13 and 14 twice, then repeat Row 13 once **more**.

Rows 20-27: Repeat Rows 12-19.

Row 28: P2, (K2, P2) 1{1-0-0} time(s), (C6B, P2) 0{1-0-0} time(s) (C6F, P2) 1{1-0-1} time(s), ★ (C6B, P2) twice, C6F, P2; repeat from ★ 1{1-2-3} time(s) **more**, (C6B, P2) 0{1-2-0} time(s), (K2, P2) 1{1-0-0} time(s).

Row 29: K2, (P2, K2) across.

Row 30: P2, (K2, P2) across.

Rows 31-35: Repeat Rows 29 and 30 twice, then repeat Row 29 once **more**.

Rows 36-43: Repeat Rows 28-35.

Rows 44-75: Repeat Rows 12-19, 4 times.

Row 76: P2, (K2, P2) 2{1-2-1} time(s), C6B, P2, (K2, P2, C6B, P2) 1{2-2-3} time(s), C6F, P2, (C6B, P2, K2, P2) 2{3-3-4} times, (K2, P2) 1{0-1-0} time(s).

Row 77: K2, (P2, K2) across.

Row 78: P2, (K2, P2) across.

Rows 79-83: Repeat Rows 77 and 78 twice, then repeat Row 77 once **more**.

Rows 84 thru 102{102-110-110}: Repeat Rows 12-19, 2{2-3-3} times; then repeat Rows 12-14 once **more**.

Last Row: Bind off first 13{19-23-29} sts in **knit**, work across in established pattern until there are 40{44-44-48} sts on the right knitting needle, slip 40{44-44-48} sts just worked onto a st holder; bind off the remaining sts in **knit**.

Sew shoulder seams.

SLEEVE

Place a marker on **both** sides of **both** pieces, 7{7¹⁄₂-8-8¹⁄₂}"/18{19-20.5-21.5} cm down from shoulder seams.

With **right** side facing, pick up 51{55-58-61} sts between markers *(Figs. 9a & b, page 93)*.

Row 1: Purl across.

Row 2 (Right side)**:** Knit across.

Rows 3-13: Repeat Rows 1 and 2, 5 times; then repeat Row 1 once **more**.

Row 14 (Decrease row)**:** K1, SSK *(Figs. 5a-c, page 92)*, knit across to last 3 sts, K2 tog *(Fig. 3, page 92)*, K1: 49{53-56-59} sts.

Continue in Stockinette Stitch, decreasing one st at **each** edge in same manner, every 14th row, 4{0-0-0} times; then decrease every 12th row, 2{5-2-2} times; then decrease every 10th row, 0{2-6-6} times: 37{39-40-43} sts.

Work even until Sleeve measures approximately 23{23-24-24}"/58.5{58.5-61-61} cm, ending by working a **purl** row.

Bind off all sts **loosely** in **knit**.

Repeat for second Sleeve.

Instructions continued on page 25.

FINISHING
NECK RIBBING

Rnd 1: With **right** side facing and using double-pointed knitting needles, slip 40{44-44-48} sts from first st holder onto empty knitting needle and work across in established pattern; slip 40{44-44-48} sts from second st holder onto empty knitting needle and work across in established pattern; place a marker to mark the beginning of the rnd *(see **Knitting in the Round and Markers, pages 91 and 92**)*: 80{88-88-96} sts.

Work in K2, P2 ribbing around until ribbing measures approximately 7" (18 cm).

Bind off all sts **very loosely** in ribbing.

Sew underarm and sides in one continuous seam.

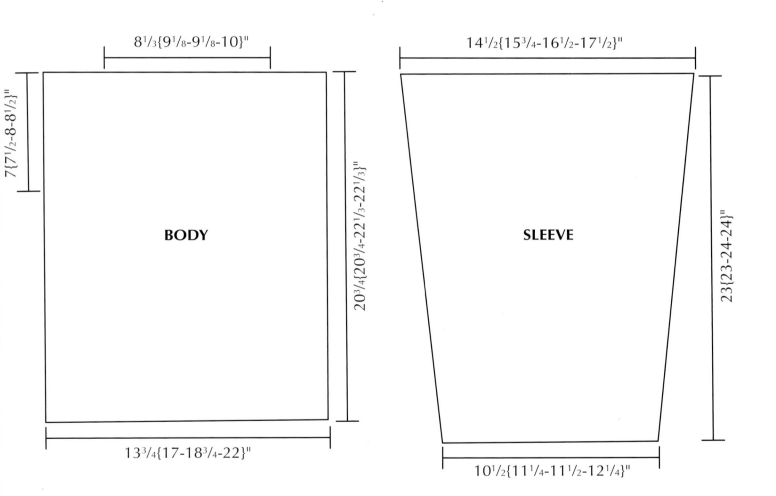

BODY

8¹/₃{9¹/₈-9¹/₈-10}"

7{7¹/₂-8-8¹/₂}"

20³/₄{20³/₄-22¹/₃-22¹/₃}"

13³/₄{17-18³/₄-22}"

SLEEVE

14¹/₂{15³/₄-16¹/₂-17¹/₂}"

23{23-24-24}"

10¹/₂{11¹/₄-11¹/₂-12¹/₄}"

Note: Sweater includes two edge stitches.

Short Sleeve Top

Shown on pages 26 and 27.

■■■□ INTERMEDIATE

Size	Finished Chest Measurement
X-Small	30" (76 cm)
Small	33" (84 cm)
Medium	36" (91.5 cm)
Large	42" (106.5 cm)

Size Note: Instructions are written for size X-Small with sizes Small, Medium and Large in braces { }. Instructions will be easier to read if you circle all the numbers pertaining to your size. If only one number is given, it applies to all sizes.

MATERIALS

Medium Weight Yarn 【MEDIUM 4】
[2¹/₂ ounces, 222 yards
(70 grams, 202 meters) per skein]:
  3{4-4-4} skeins
29" (73.5 cm) Circular knitting needle,
  size 10¹/₂ (6.5 mm) **or** size needed for gauge
Straight knitting needles, size 10¹/₂ (6.5 mm)
  or size needed for gauge
Double-pointed knitting needles, size 10¹/₂
  (6.5 mm) **or** size needed for gauge
Cable needle
Stitch holders - 4
Marker
Crochet hook, sizes F (3.75 cm) **and** K (6.5 mm)
Straight pins (to attach Collar)

GAUGE: With circular or straight knitting needles,
in Lattice Pattern
(Rnds 1-60 slightly stretched),
16 sts and 21 rows/rnds = 4" (10 cm)
With double-pointed knitting needles,
in Stockinette Stitch,
16 sts and 20 rows/rnds = 4" (10 cm)

STITCH GUIDE

FRONT CABLE *(abbreviated FC)*
  (uses next 6 sts)
Slip next 3 sts onto cable needle and hold at
front of work, K3 from left needle, K3 from
cable needle.

BACK CABLE *(abbreviated BC)*
  (uses next 6 sts)
Slip next 3 sts onto cable needle and hold at
back of work, K3 from left needle, K3 from
cable needle.

Body is worked in one piece to underarm.

BODY

With circular knitting needle, cast on
120{132-144-168} sts; place a marker to mark the
beginning of the rnd *(see Knitting in the Round and
Markers, pages 91 and 92)*.

Rnds 1-4: Knit around.

Rnd 5: FC around.

Rnds 6-10: Knit around.

Rnd 11: K3, BC around to last 3 sts, slip last 3 sts onto cable needle and hold in **back** of work, remove marker, K3 from left needle, place marker to mark the beginning of the next rnd, K3 from cable needle *(these are the first 3 sts of the next rnd)*.

Rnd 12: Knit around.

Rnds 13-60: Repeat Rows 1-12, 4 times.

Rnds 61-68: Knit around.

Rnd 69: BC around.

Rnds 70-76: Knit around.

Rnd 77: BC around.

Rnds 78-80: Knit around.

FRONT

Row 1 (Right side)**:** With straight knitting needles, knit 60{66-72-84} sts, leave remaining sts unworked on circular knitting needle (Back).

Row 2: Purl across.

Row 3: Knit across.

Row 4: Purl across.

Row 5: BC across.

Rows 6-14: Repeat Rows 2 and 3, 4 times; then repeat Row 2 once **more**.

Row 15: BC across.

Work even in Stockinette Stitch **(knit one row, purl one row)** until Front measures approximately 7{7$\frac{1}{2}$-8-8$\frac{1}{2}$}"/18{19-20.5-21.5} cm from underarm, ending by working a **purl** row.

Last Row: Knit 13{15-17-22} sts, slip sts just knit onto a st holder; bind off center 34{36-38-40} sts; knit across remaining sts, slip sts just knit onto a second st holder: 13{15-17-22} sts on **each** st holder.

BACK

Row 1: With **right** side facing, using straight knitting needles, and working across sts on circular knitting needle, knit across: 60{66-72-84} sts.

Beginning with Row 2, complete same as Front.

Slip sts from Front and Back right shoulder st holders onto double-pointed knitting needles. Work 3-Needle Bind off *(Fig. 8, page 93)*.

Repeat for left shoulder.

SLEEVE
BODY

With **right** side facing, using double-pointed knitting needles, and beginning at underarm, pick up 28{30-32-34} sts *(Figs. 9a & b, page 93)* to shoulder, pick up 28{30-32-34} sts to underarm; place a marker to mark the beginning of the rnd: 56{60-64-68} sts.

Knit every rnd until Sleeve measures approximately 4$\frac{1}{2}$" (11.5 cm) **or to desired length**.

Bind off all sts in **knit**, leaving last st on knitting needle; do **not** cut yarn.

CROCHET EDGING
See Crochet Stitches, page 94.

With **right** side facing, transfer st from knitting needle onto the smaller size crochet hook; ch 1, sc in each bound-off st around; join with slip st to first sc, finish off.

Repeat for second Sleeve.

Instructions continued on page 31.

COLLAR

With straight knitting needles, cast on 84{90-90-96} sts.

Row 1 (Right side)**:** Knit across.

Row 2: Purl across.

Rows 3 and 4: Repeat Rows 1 and 2.

Row 5: FC across.

Row 6: Purl across.

Rows 7-10: Repeat Rows 1 and 2 twice.

Row 11: K3, BC across to last 3 sts, K3.

Row 12: Purl across.

Rows 13-20: Repeat Rows 1-8.

Bind off all sts **loosely.**

FINISHING
COLLAR EDGING

Row 1: With **right** side facing and using the larger size crochet hook, join yarn with slip st in end of Row 1; sc evenly across end of rows to next corner, 3 sc in corner; sc in back loop only of each bound-off st across to next corner, 3 sc in corner, sc evenly across end of rows; do **not** work across cast on edge, finish off.

Row 2: With **right** side facing, using the larger size crochet hook, and working in Back Loops Only **(Fig. 16, page 94)**, join yarn with sc in first sc; sc in each sc across working 3 sc in each corner; do **not** finish off.

With **right** side of Collar and **wrong** side of top together, pin center of Collar to center of back neck edge. Pin remainder of Collar around neck edge, overlapping 4¹/₂-5" (11.5-12.5 cm) in Front. With **wrong** side of Collar facing, continue to sc around entire neck edge, working through all thicknesses to attach Collar; join with slip st to first sc, finish off.

BODY EDGING

With **right** side facing and using the larger size crochet hook, join yarn with sc in any st of cast on; skip next st, (sc in next st, skip next st) around; join with slip st to first sc, finish off.

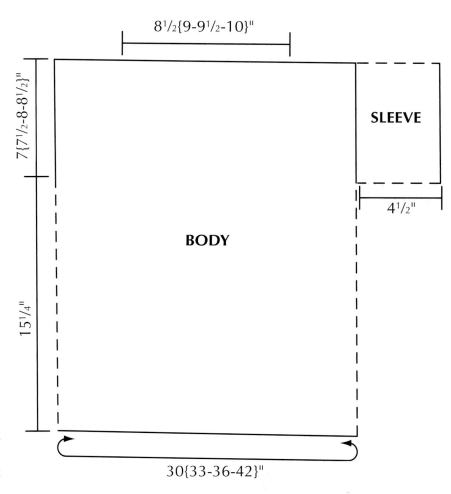

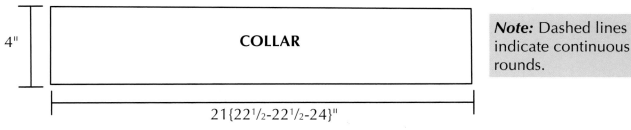

Note: Dashed lines indicate continuous rounds.

Halter

Shown on pages 32 and 33.

⬤⬛⬛▢ INTERMEDIATE

Size	Finished Chest Measurement
X-Small	21" (53.5 cm)
Small	28" (71 cm)
Medium	35" (89 cm)
Large	42" (106.5 cm)

Size Note: Instructions are written for size X-Small with sizes Small, Medium and Large in braces { }. Instructions will be easier to read if you circle all the numbers pertaining to your size. If only one number is given, it applies to all sizes.

MATERIALS

DK Weight Yarn
[1³/₄ ounces, 130 yards
(50 grams, 119 meters) per skein]:
   7{9-11-13} skeins
24-29" (61-73.5 cm) Circular knitting needle,
   size 8 (5 mm) **or** size needed for gauge
Straight knitting needles, size 8 (5 mm) **or**
   size needed for gauge
Cable needle
Crochet hook, size H (5 mm)
Marker
Straight pins (to attach Collar)

GAUGE: With two strands of yarn held together,
in pattern (slightly stretched),
16 sts = 3¹/₂" (9 cm);
23 rows/rnds = 4" (10 cm)

STITCH GUIDE

CABLE 6 FRONT *(abbreviated C6F)*
(uses next 6 sts)
Slip next 4 sts onto cable needle and hold at **front** of work, K2 from left needle, slip last 2 sts from cable needle **back** to left needle and purl them, then K2 from cable needle.

Body is worked in one piece to the underarm.

BODY

With circular knitting needle and two strands of yarn held together, cast on 96{128-160-192} sts; place a marker to mark the beginning of the rnd *(see Knitting in the Round and Markers, pages 91 and 92).*

Rnds 1-14: (K2, P2) around.

Rnd 15: ★ (K2, P2) twice, C6F, P2; repeat from ★ around.

Rnds 16-18: (K2, P2) around.

Rnd 19: ★ C6F, P2, (K2, P2) twice; repeat from ★ around.

Rnds 20-22: (K2, P2) around.

Rnd 23: ★ (K2, P2) twice, C6F, P2; repeat from ★ around.

Rnds 24-26: (K2, P2) around.

Rnd 27: ★ C6F, P2, (K2, P2) twice; repeat from ★ around.

Rnds 28-30: (K2, P2) around.

Rnd 31: ★ (K2, P2) twice, C6F, P2; repeat from ★ around.

Rnds 32-49: (K2, P2) around.

Rnds 50-84: Repeat Rnds 15-49.

FRONT
Row 1 (Right side)**:** Bind off first 38{54-70-86} sts in **knit** (Back), P1, C6F, P2, ★ (K2, P2) twice, C6F, P2; repeat from ★ across: 58{74-90-106} sts.

Row 2: K2, (P2, K2) across.

Row 3: P2, (K2, P2) across.

Row 4: K2, (P2, K2) across.

Row 5: P2, (K2, P2) twice, ★ C6F, P2, (K2, P2) twice; repeat from ★ across.

Row 6: K2, (P2, K2) across.

Row 7: P2, (K2, P2) across.

Row 8: K2, (P2, K2) across.

Row 9: P2, C6F, P2, ★ (K2, P2) twice, C6F, P2; repeat from ★ across.

Rows 10-17: Repeat Rows 2-9.

Row 18: K2, (P2, K2) across.

Row 19: P2, (K2, P2) across.

Repeat Rows 18 and 19 until Front measures approximately 7$\frac{1}{2}${8-8$\frac{1}{2}$-9}"/19{20.5-21.5-23} cm **or to desired length**, ending by working Row 18.

Bind off all sts in **knit**.

FINISHING
COLLAR
With two strands of yarn held together, cast on 9 sts.

Work in Stockinette Stitch **(knit one row, purl one row)** until piece measures approximately 36" (91.5 cm) from cast on edge, ending by working a **purl** row.

Bind off all sts in **knit**, leaving last st on knitting needle; do **not** cut yarn.

See Crochet Stitches, page 94.

Edging Rnd: With **right** side facing, transfer st from knitting needle onto the crochet hook; ch 1, sc in end of every other row across to next corner, 3 sc in corner, sc in each cast on st across to next corner, 3 sc in corner, sc in end of every other row across to next corner, 3 sc in corner, sc in each bound-off st across; join with slip st to first sc, finish off.

Instructions continued on page 37.

With **wrong** sides together, pin the Collar to the Front matching the center of Collar to center of Front.

With **right** side of Front toward you, using two strands of yarn held together and the crochet hook, join yarn with sc through **both** pieces at beginning of Front bind off *(see Joining With Sc, page 94)*; sc evenly across, working through **both** pieces to attach Collar to Front; finish off.

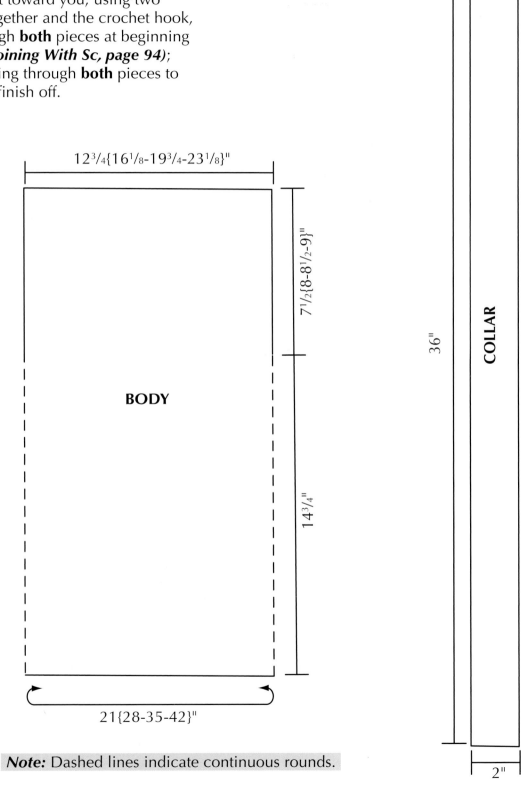

12³/₄{16¹/₈-19³/₄-23¹/₈}"

7¹/₂{8-8¹/₂-9}"

BODY

14³/₄"

21{28-35-42}"

36"

COLLAR

2"

Note: Dashed lines indicate continuous rounds.

Sleeveless Top

Shown on pages 38 and 39.

■■■□ INTERMEDIATE

Size	Finished Chest Measurement
Small	26" (66 cm)
Medium	34¹/₂" (87.5 cm)
Large	43" (109 cm)

Size Note: Instructions are written for size Small with sizes Medium and Large in braces { }. Instructions will be easier to read if you circle all the numbers pertaining to your size. If only one number is given, it applies to all sizes.

MATERIALS

Bulky Weight Yarn 🕸5 BULKY
[3 ounces, 135 yards
(85 grams, 123 meters) per skein]:
 4{6-7} skeins
29" (73.5 cm) Circular knitting needle,
 size 11 (8 mm) **or** size needed for gauge
Straight knitting needles, size 11 (8 mm)
Cable needle
Markers
Crochet hook, size J (6 mm)
Yarn needle

GAUGE: In pattern (slightly stretched),
 22 sts = 4³/₄" (12 cm);
 24 rows/rnds = 6¹/₄" (10 cm)

STITCH GUIDE

CABLE 7 FRONT *(abbreviated C7F)*
 (uses next 7 sts)
Slip next 4 sts onto cable needle and hold at **front** of work, (K1, P1, K1) from left needle, slip last st on cable needle **back** to left needle and purl it, then (K1, P1, K1) from cable needle.

CABLE 7 BACK *(abbreviated C7B)*
 (uses next 7 sts)
Slip next 4 sts onto cable needle and hold at **back** of work, (K1, P1, K1) from left needle, slip last st on cable needle **back** to left needle and purl it, then (K1, P1, K1) from cable needle.

CABLE 9 FRONT *(abbreviated C9F)*
 (uses next 9 sts)
Slip next 6 sts onto cable needle and hold at **front** of work, (K1, P1, K1) from left needle, slip **first** 3 sts from cable needle **back** to left needle, (P1, K1, P1) from cable needle, (K1, P1, K1) from left needle.

Body is worked in one piece to the underarm.

BODY

With circular knitting needle, cast on 120{160-200} sts; place a marker to mark the beginning of the rnd (see Knitting in the Round and Markers, pages 91 and 92).

Rnds 1-6: (K1, P1) around.

Rnd 7 (Right side)**:** ★ K1, P1, work C7F, P1, K1, P1, work C7B, P1; repeat from ★ around.

Rnd 8: (K1, P1) around.

Rnd 9: ★ (K1, P1) 3 times, work C9F, P1, (K1, P1) twice; repeat from ★ around.

Rnd 10: (K1, P1) around.

Rnd 11: ★ K1, P1, work C7B, P1, K1, P1, work C7F, P1; repeat from ★ around.

Rnds 12 thru 17{19-19}: (K1, P1) around.

Rnd 18{20-20}: (K1, P1) around to last 10 sts, place marker to mark beginning of rnd for next 12{14-14} rnds.

Remove the previous beginning of the rnd marker when you reach it on the next rnd.

Rnd 19{21-21}: ★ K1, P1, work C7F, P1, K1, P1, work C7B, P1; repeat from ★ around.

Rnd 20{22-22}: (K1, P1) around.

Rnd 21{23-23}: ★ (K1, P1) 3 times, work C9F, P1, (K1, P1) twice; repeat from ★ around.

Rnd 22{24-24}: (K1, P1) around.

Rnd 23{25-25}: ★ K1, P1, work C7B, P1, K1, P1, work C7F, P1; repeat from ★ around.

Rnds 24{26-26} thru 29{33-33}: (K1, P1) around.

Rnd 30{34-34}: (K1, P1) around; remove the beginning of the rnd marker, (K1, P1) 5 times, place a marker to mark the beginning of the rnd.

Next 30{36-36} Rnds: Repeat Rnds 7 thru 30{34-34} once, then repeat Rnds 7 thru 12{14-14} once **more**.

FRONT

Row 1 (Right side)**:** With straight knitting needles, bind off one st, (K1, P1) 29{39-49} times, leave remaining 60{80-100} sts unworked on circular knitting needle (Back): 59{79-99} sts.

Row 2: K1, (P1, K1) across.

Row 3: P1, (K1, P1) across.

Rows 4-6: Repeat Rows 2 and 3 once, then repeat Row 2 once **more**.

Row 7: ★ † P1, work C7B, P1, K1, P1, work C7F, P1 †, K1; repeat from ★ 1{2-3} time(s), then repeat from † to † once **more**.

Row 8: K1, (P1, K1) across.

Row 9: P1, (K1, P1) 7 times, work C9F, ★ P1, (K1, P1) 5 times, work C9F; repeat from ★ 0{1-2} time(s) **more (see Zeros, page 92)**, P1, (K1, P1) 7 times.

Row 10: K1, (P1, K1) across.

Row 11: ★ † P1, work C7F, P1, K1, P1, work C7B, P1 †, K1; repeat from ★ 1{2-3} times **more**, then repeat from † to † once.

Row 12: K1, (P1, K1) across.

Row 13: P1, (K1, P1) across.

Rows 14 thru 18{20-20}: Repeat Rows 12 and 13, 2{3-3} times; then repeat Row 12 once **more**.

Row 19{21-21}: ★ † P1, work C7F, P1, K1, P1, work C7B, P1 †, K1; repeat from ★ 1{2-3} time(s) **more**, then repeat from † to † once.

Row 20{22-22}: K1, (P1, K1) across.

Instructions continued on page 43.

Row 21{23-23}: P1, (K1, P1) twice, work C9F, ★ P1, (K1, P1) 5 times, work C9F; repeat from ★ 1{2-3} time(s) **more**, P1, (K1, P1) twice.

Row 22{24-24}: K1, (P1, K1) across.

Row 23{25-25}: ★ † P1, work C7B, P1, K1, P1, work C7F, P1 †, K1; repeat from ★ 1{2-3} time(s) **more**, then repeat from † to † once.

Row 24{26-26}: K1, (P1, K1) across.

Row 25{27-27}: P1, (K1, P1) across.

Next 3{5-5} Rows: Repeat Rows 24{26-26} and 25{27-27}, 1{2-2} time(s); then repeat Row 24{26-26} once **more**.

Bind off all sts in pattern.

BACK
Row 1: With **right** side facing, using straight knitting needles, and working across sts on circular knitting needle, bind off one st, (K1, P1) across: 59{79-99} sts.

Complete same as Front.

FINISHING
Sew each shoulder seam leaving a(n) 8{9-10}"/ 20.5-{23-25.5} cm neck opening.

NECK EDGING
See Crochet Stitches, page 94.

With **right** side facing and using the crochet hook, join yarn with sc in any shoulder seam *(see Joining With Sc, page 94)*; sc in each st and seam around neck edge; join with slip st to first sc, finish off.

ARMHOLE EDGING
With **right** side facing and using the crochet hook, join yarn with sc in bound-off st at underarm; sc evenly around armhole edge; join with slip st to first sc, finish off.

Repeat around second Armhole.

KNOTS
With **right** side of cable facing, bring threaded yarn needle up at 1, go down at 2 and come up at 3 *(Fig. A)*, go down at 4. On wrong side of cable, tie ends in a secure knot.

Fig. A

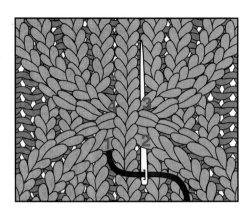

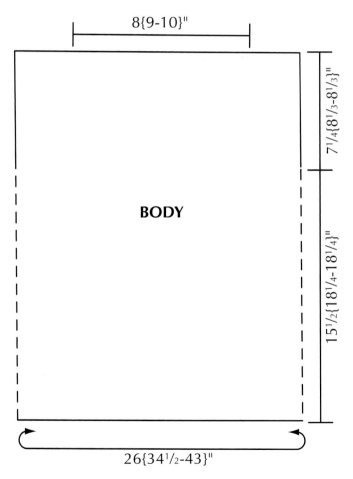

8{9-10}"

7¼{8⅓-8⅓}"

BODY

15½{18¼-18¼}"

26{34½-43}"

Note: Vertical measurements are given **before** "knots" have been tied. Dashed lines indicate continuous rounds.

Tunic

Shown on pages 44 and 45.

●●■□ INTERMEDIATE

Size	Finished Chest Measurement
X-Small	30" (76 cm)
Small	33" (84 cm)
Medium	36" (91.5 cm)
Large	42" (106.5 cm)

Size Note: Instructions are written for size X-Small with sizes Small, Medium and Large in braces { }. Instructions will be easier to read if you circle all the numbers pertaining to your size. If only one number is given, it applies to all sizes.

MATERIALS

Medium Weight Yarn
[1³/₄ ounces, 165 yards
(50 grams, 150 meters) per skein]:
   8{9-10-11} skeins
29" (73.5 cm) Circular knitting needle,
   sizes 10¹/₂ (6.5 mm) **and** 11 (8 mm)
   or sizes needed for gauge
Straight knitting needles, size 11 (8 mm)
   or size needed for gauge
Double-pointed knitting needles,
   size 10¹/₂ (6.5 mm) **or** size needed for gauge
Cable needle

Marker
Crochet hook, size J (6 mm)
Yarn needle

GAUGE: In Stockinette Stitch,
   with larger size knitting needles,
   8 sts and 10 rows/rnds = 3" (7.5 cm)
   with smaller size knitting needles,
   13 sts and 16 rows/rnds = 4" (10 cm)

STITCH GUIDE

FRONT CABLE *(abbreviated FC)*
   (uses next 6 sts)
Slip next 3 sts onto cable needle and hold at **front** of work, K3 from left needle, K3 from cable needle.

BACK CABLE *(abbreviated BC)*
   (uses next 6 sts)
Slip next 3 sts onto cable needle and hold at **back** of work, K3 from left needle, K3 from cable needle.

CABLE 7 FRONT *(abbreviated C7F)*
   (uses next 7 sts)
Slip next 4 sts onto cable needle and hold at **front** of work, K3 from left needle, slip last st from cable needle **back** to left needle and purl it, then K3 from cable needle.

FRONT & BACK

The Cable Strip is worked first and joined to form a ring. Stitches are picked up along one edge and worked in pattern to form the lower section of the Front and Back without a seam. Stitches are picked up along the opposite edge to be worked in a cable pattern to form the waist and then continued up in pattern to the underarm. Front and Back are worked separately at this point to form raglan shaping.

CABLE STRIP

With larger size circular knitting needle and leaving a long end for sewing, cast on 15 sts.

Row 1: K3, P9, K3.

Row 2 (Right side)**:** P3, FC, K3, P3.

Row 3: K3, P9, K3.

Row 4: P3, K9, P3.

Row 5: K3, P9, K3.

Row 6: P3, K3, BC, P3.

Row 7: K3, P9, K3.

Row 8: P3, K9, P3.

Rows 9 thru 80{88-96-112}: Repeat Rows 1-8, 9{10-11-13} times.

Bind off all sts in pattern, then pull yarn through last st **without** cutting yarn (it will be used for Lower Edge).

Fold Cable Strip in half with **right** sides together; using long yarn end, sew ends of Cable Strip together.

LOWER EDGE

With **right** side facing, using smaller size circular knitting needle, and still attached working yarn, pick up a st in end of each row along Cable Strip *(Fig. 9a, page 93)*; place a marker to mark the beginning of the rnd *(see Knitting in the Round and Markers, pages 91 and 92)*: 80{88-96-112} sts.

Rnds 1-4: Knit around.

Rnds 5 and 6: Purl around.

Rnds 7-11: Knit around.

Change to size larger size circular knitting needle.

Rnds 12-27: Repeat Rnds 5-11 twice, then repeat Rnds 5 and 6 once **more**.

Rnds 28 and 29: Knit around.

Bind off all sts in **knit**, leaving last st on knitting needle; do **not** cut yarn.

CROCHET EDGING
See Crochet Stitches, page 94.

Rnd 1: With **right** side facing, transfer st from knitting needle onto the crochet hook; ch 1, sc in each st around; join with slip st to first sc.

Rnds 2 and 3: Ch 1, sc in each sc around; join with slip st to first sc.

Rnd 4: Ch 1, sc in Back Loop Only of each sc around *(Fig. 16, page 94)*; join with slip st to **both** loops of first sc, finish off.

WAIST

With **right** side facing, using smaller size circular knitting needle, and beginning at seam, pick up a st in end of each row along Cable Strip, opposite Lower Edge; place a marker to mark the beginning of the rnd: 80{88-96-112} sts.

Rnds 1-4: Knit around.

Rnds 5-9: (P1, K3) around.

Rnd 10: (P1, C7F) around.

Rnds 11-17: (P1, K3) around.

Rnds 18-24: Repeat Rnds 10-16.

Instructions continued on page 48.

Rnds 25-27: Knit around.

YOKE
Change to larger size circular knitting needle.

Rnds 1 and 2: Purl around.

Rnds 3-7: Knit around.

Rnds 8-21: Repeat Rnds 1-7 twice.

BACK RAGLAN SHAPING
Row 1 (Decrease row)**:** With straight knitting needles, K1, SSK *(Figs. 5a-c, page 92)*, P 34{38-42-50}, K2 tog *(Fig. 3, page 92)*, K1, leave remaining 40{44-48-56} sts on circular knitting needle (Front): 38{42-46-54} sts.

Row 2: P2, knit across to last 2 sts, P2.

Row 3 (Decrease row)**:** K1, SSK, knit across to last 3 sts, K2 tog, K1: 36{40-44-52} sts.

Row 4: Purl across.

Rows 5-7: Repeat Rows 3 and 4 once, then repeat Row 3 once **more**: 32{36-40-48} sts.

Row 8: P2, knit across to last 2 sts, P2.

Row 9 (Decrease row)**:** K1, SSK, purl across to last 3 sts, K2 tog, K1: 30{34-38-46} sts.

Row 10: Purl across.

Rows 11-14: Repeat Rows 3 and 4 twice: 26{30-34-42} sts.

Row 15 (Decrease row)**:** K1, SSK, purl across to last 3 sts, K2 tog, K1: 24{28-32-40} sts.

Rows 16 thru 24{28-29-29}: Repeat Rows 2 thru 10{14-15-15}: 16{16-18-26} sts.

SIZE MEDIUM ONLY - Row 30: P2, knit across to last 2 sts, P2.

SIZE LARGE ONLY - Rows 30-38: Repeat Rows 2-10: 18 sts.

ALL SIZES: Bind off remaining sts **loosely**.

FRONT RAGLAN SHAPING
Row 1 (Decrease row)**:** With **right** side facing, using straight knitting needles, and working across sts on circular knitting needle, K1, SSK, purl across to last 3 sts, K2 tog, K1: 38{42-46-54} sts.

Rows 2 thru 16{20-22-30}: Work same as Back: 24{24-26-26} sts.

Neck Shaping
Row 1: K1, SSK, K3, K2 tog, K1, bind off next 6{6-8-8} sts, SSK, K3, K2 tog, K1: 7 sts **each** side.

Both sides of the Neck are worked at the same time, using a separate yarn for **each** side.

Row 2: Purl across; with second yarn, purl across.

Row 3: K1, SSK, K1, K2 tog, K1; with second yarn, K1, SSK, K1, K2 tog, K1: 5 sts **each** side.

Row 4: Purl across; with second yarn, purl across.

Row 5: K1, SSK, K2 tog; with second yarn, SSK, K2 tog, K1: 3 sts **each** side.

Row 6: Purl across; with second yarn, purl across.

Row 7: K1, K2 tog; with second yarn, SSK, K1: 2 sts **each** side.

Row 8: P2 tog *(Fig. 4, page 92)*; with second yarn, P2 tog: one st **each** side.

Finish off.

SLEEVE (Make 2)
CABLE STRIP
Rows 1 thru 40{40-48-48}: Work same as Front and Back.

Bind off all sts in pattern, then pull yarn through last st **without** cutting yarn (it will be used for Crochet Edging).

Fold Cable Strip in half with **right** sides together; using long yarn end, sew ends of Cable Strip together.

CROCHET EDGING
Rnd 1: With **right** side facing, using the crochet hook and still attached working yarn, pull up a loop in next row; ch 1, sc in same row and in each row around; join with slip st to first sc: 40{40-48-48} sc.

Rnd 2: Ch 1, sc in Back Loop Only of each sc around; join with slip st to **both** loops of first sc, finish off.

BODY
Rnd 1: With **right** side facing, using double-pointed knitting needles and beginning at seam, pick up a st in end of each row along Cable Strip, opposite Crochet Edging; dividing the sts evenly on double-pointed knitting needles; place a marker to mark the beginning of the rnd: 40{40-48-48} sts.

Knit every rnd until Sleeve measures approximately 19{18^1/$_4$-17^1/$_2$-16}"/48.5{46.5-44.5-40.5} cm from edge.

RAGLAN SHAPING
Begin working in rows.

Row 1 (Decrease row)**:** K1, SSK, knit around to last 3 sts before marker, K2 tog, K1; remove marker: 38{38-46-46} sts.

Row 2: Purl across.

Row 3: K1, SSK, knit across to last 3 sts, K2 tog, K1: 36{36-44-44} sts.

Rows 4 thru 14{22-18-34}: Repeat Rows 2 and 3, 5{9-7-15} times; then repeat Row 2 once **more**: 26{18-30-14} sts.

Next Decrease Row: K1, SSK, knit across to last 3 sts, K2 tog, K1: 24{16-28-12} sts.

Next Decrease Row: P1, P2 tog, purl across to last 3 sts, SSP **(Fig. 6, page 92)**, P1: 22{14-26-10} sts.

Repeat last 2 decrease rows, 4{2-5-1} time(s): 6 sts.

Bind off remaining sts in **knit**.

COLLAR
Collar is worked as a strip, joined, then attached to neck edge.

CABLE STRIP
Using larger size circular knitting needle and leaving a 40" (101.5 cm) end for sewing, cast on 23 sts.

Row 1: K 11, P9, K3.

Row 2 (Right side)**:** P3, FC, K3, P 11.

Row 3: K 11, P9, K3.

Row 4: P3, K9, P 11.

Row 5: K 11, P9, K3.

Row 6: P3, K3, BC, P 11.

Row 7: K 11, P9, K3.

Row 8: P3, K9, P 11.

Rows 9 thru 64{64-72-72}: Repeat Rows 1-8, 7{7-8-8} times.

Bind off all sts in pattern, then pull yarn through last st **without** cutting yarn (it will be used for Crochet Edging).

Instructions continued on page 51.

Fold Cable Strip in half with **right** sides together; using long yarn end, sew ends of Cable Strip together.

CROCHET EDGING

Rnd 1: With **right** side facing, using the crochet hook and still attached working yarn, pull up a loop in next row; ch 1, sc in same row and in each row around; join with slip st to first sc.

Rnd 2: Ch 1, sc in Back Loop Only of each sc around; join with slip st to both **loops** of first sc, finish off.

FINISHING

Weave Sleeves to Front and Back *(Fig. 10, page 93)*.

To maintain elasticity, Collar is crocheted to neck edge as follows:
With **right** side of Collar facing **wrong** side of Front and Back, and having seam at Center Back, pin Collar edge opposite Crochet Edging in place along neck edge easing Collar to fit.

Using the crochet hook and working through **both** layers, join yarn with slip st in st in Collar seam; ch 1, sc evenly around; join with slip st to first sc, finish off.

Turn Collar in half to **right** side.

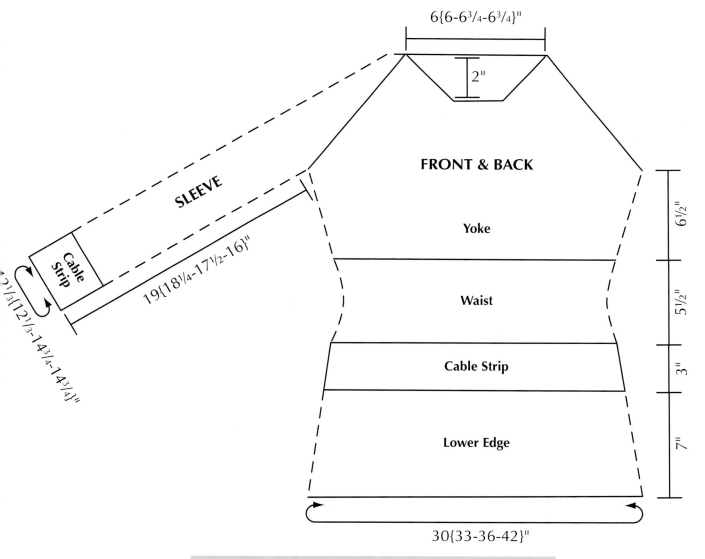

Note: Dashed lines indicate continuous rounds.

Split Neck Shell

Shown on pages 52 and 53.

■■■□ INTERMEDIATE

Size	Finished Chest Measurement
X-Small	31$^{1}/_{2}$" (80 cm)
Small	36" (91.5 cm)
Medium	40$^{1}/_{2}$" (103 cm)
Large	45" (114.5 cm)

Size Note: Instructions are written for size X-Small with sizes Small, Medium and Large in braces { }. Instructions will be easier to read if you circle all the numbers pertaining to your size. If only one number is given, it applies to all sizes.

MATERIALS

Bulky Weight Yarn
[3 ounces, 135 yards
(85 grams, 123 meters) per skein]:
  5{6-6-7} skeins
29" (73.5 cm) Circular knitting needle,
  size 11 (8 mm) **or** size needed for gauge
Straight knitting needles, size 11 (8 mm)
Cable needle
Stitch holders - 2
Markers
Crochet hook, size J (6 mm)

GAUGE: In Cable pattern (slightly stretched),
16 sts (4 cables) = 4$^{1}/_{2}$" (11.5 cm);
12 rows/rnds (3 repeats) = 3$^{1}/_{2}$" (9 cm)

STITCH GUIDE

CABLE 3 FRONT *(abbreviated C3F)*
  (uses next 3 sts)
Slip next 2 sts onto cable needle and hold at **front** of work, K1 from left needle, slip last st from cable needle **back** to left needle and purl it, then K1 from cable needle.
CABLE 3 BACK *(abbreviated C3B)*
  (uses next 3 sts)
Slip next 2 sts onto cable needle and hold at **back** of work, K1 from left needle, slip last st from cable needle **back** to left needle and purl it, then K1 from cable needle.

Body is worked in one piece to the underarm.

BODY
RIBBING

With circular knitting needle, cast on 112{128-144-160} sts; place a marker to mark the beginning of the rnd *(see Knitting in the Round and Markers, pages 91 and 92)*.

Being careful not to twist sts around knitting needle, work in K1, P1 ribbing for 3$^{1}/_{2}$" (9 cm).

LATTICE PATTERN

Rnd 1: (C3F, P1) around.

Rnd 2: (K1, P1) around to last 2 sts, slip last 2 sts onto cable needle and hold at **back** of work, remove marker, K1 from left needle, slip last st from cable needle **back** to left needle and purl it, replace marker.

Rnd 3: K1 from cable needle, P1, (C3B, P1) around to last 2 sts, K1, P1.

Rnd 4: (K1, P1) around.

Repeat Rnds 1-4 for Lattice pattern for 4¹/₂" (11.5 cm), ending by working Rnd 1 or Rnd 3.

RIBBING

Work in K1, P1 ribbing for 3" (7.5 cm).

CABLE PATTERN

Rnd 1: (C3F, P1) around.

Rnds 2-4: (K1, P1) around.

Rnds 5-14: Repeat Rnds 1-4 twice, then repeat Rnds 1 and 2 once **more**.

BACK

Row 1 (Right side)**:** With straight knitting needles, bind off 4 sts, P1, (K1, P1) 25{29-33-37} times, leave remaining sts unworked on circular knitting needle (Front): 52{60-68-76} sts.

Row 2: Bind off 4 sts, P1, (K1, P1) across: 48{56-64-72} sts.

Row 3: (C3F, P1) across.

Rows 4-6: (K1, P1) across.

Next 5{5-9-9} Rows: Repeat Rows 3-6, 1{1-2-2} time(s); then repeat Row 3 once **more**.

Work in K1, P1 ribbing until Back measures approximately 6{6¹/₂-7-7¹/₂}"/15{16.5-18-19} cm, ending by working a **wrong** side row.

Slip sts onto a st holder; cut yarn.

FRONT

Row 1: With **right** side facing, using straight knitting needles, and working across sts on circular knitting needle, bind off 4 sts, P1, (K1, P1) across: 52{60-68-76} sts.

Beginning with Row 2, complete same as Back, leaving sts on knitting needle; do **not** cut yarn: 48{56-64-72} sts.

SHOULDER SHAPING

Rnd 1 (Joining rnd)**:** With circular knitting needle, work in K1, P1 ribbing across Front, place a marker to mark right shoulder; with **right** side of Back facing, slip sts from st holder onto empty straight knitting needle, with circular knitting needle, work in K1, P1 ribbing across, place a marker to mark left shoulder and the beginning of the rnd: 96{112-128-144} sts.

Rnd 2: ★ K1, SSK *(Figs. 5a-c, page 92)*, (P1, K1) across to within 3 sts of next marker, K2 tog *(Fig. 3, page 93)*, P1; repeat from ★ once **more**: 92{108-124-140} sts.

Rnd 3: ★ K1, P2, K1, (P1, K1) across to within 2 sts of next marker, P2; repeat from ★ once **more**.

Rnd 4 (Decrease rnd)**:** ★ K1, SSK, (K1, P1) across to within 3 sts of next marker, K2 tog, P1; repeat from ★ once **more**: 88{104-120-136} sts.

Rnd 5: (K1, P1) around.

Rnd 6 (Decrease rnd)**:** ★ K1, SSK, (P1, K1) across to within 3 sts of next marker, K2 tog, P1; repeat from ★ once **more**: 84{100-116-132} sts.

Rnds 7-12: Repeat Rnds 3-6 once, then repeat Rnds 3 and 4 once **more**: 72{88-104-120} sts.

Instructions continued on page 57.

COLLAR
Begin working in rows on circular knitting needle.

Row 1: (K1, P1) across, removing both markers.

Rows 2-23: (K1, P1) across.

Row 24: (C3F, P1) across.

Row 25: (K1, P1) across.

Row 26 (Right side)**:** K1, P1, (C3B, P1) across to last 2 sts, K1, P1.

Row 27: (K1, P1) across.

Row 28: (C3F, P1) across.

Rows 29-32: (K1, P1) across.

Bind off all sts in established ribbing.

FINISHING
See Crochet Stitches, page 94.

COLLAR EDGING
With **right** side of Collar facing and using the crochet hook, join yarn with sc in Row 1 *(see Joining With Sc, page 94)*; sc evenly around Collar working 3 sc in each top corner; join with slip st to first sc, finish off.

ARMHOLE EDGING
With **right** side facing and using the crochet hook, join yarn with sc at the underarm; sc evenly around; join with slip st to first sc, finish off.

Repeat around second Armhole.

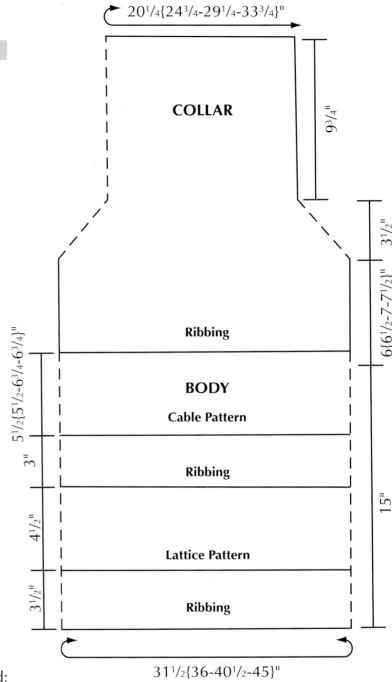

Note: Dashed lines indicate continuous rounds.

Long Sleeve Sweater

58

Long Sleeve Sweater

Shown on page 58 and 59.

◼◼◼◻ **INTERMEDIATE**

Size	Finished Chest Measurement
X-Small	28" (71 cm)
Small	32" (81.5 cm)
Medium	36" (91.5 cm)
Large	40" (101.5 cm)

Size Note: Instructions are written for size X-Small with sizes Small, Medium and Large in braces { }. Instructions will be easier to read if you circle all the numbers pertaining to your size. If only one number is given, it applies to all sizes.

MATERIALS
Bulky Weight Yarn
[3½ ounces, 164 yards
(100 grams, 150 meters) per skein]:
   12{14-16-18} skeins
29" (73.5 cm) Circular knitting needle,
   size 11 (8 mm) **or** size needed for gauge
Straight knitting needles, size 11 (8 mm)
Double-pointed knitting needles, size 11 (8 mm)
Cable needle
Stitch holders - 4
Markers
Crochet hook, size J (6 mm)

GAUGE: In Reverse Stockinette Stitch,
   12 sts and 16 rows/rnds = 4" (10 cm)
   One Cable (10 sts slightly stretched)
   = 2½"w (6.25 cm)

STITCH GUIDE

CABLE 10 FRONT *(abbreviated C10F)*
   (uses next 10 sts)
Slip next 6 sts onto cable needle and hold at **front** of work, K4 from left needle, slip last 2 sts from cable needle **back** to left needle and purl them, then K4 from cable needle.

CABLE 10 BACK *(abbreviated C10B)*
   (uses next 10 sts)
Slip next 6 sts onto cable needle and hold at **back** of work, K4 from left needle, slip last 2 sts from cable needle **back** to left needle and purl them, then K4 from cable needle.

Body is worked in one piece to underarm.

BODY
With circular knitting needle, cast on 89{101-113-125} sts; place a marker to mark the beginning of the rnd *(see Knitting in the Round and Markers, pages 91 and 92)*.

Rnds 1-11: K2, P7{9-12-14}, K4, P2, K4, P9{11-11-13}, K4, P2, K4, P7{9-12-14}, K4, P 38{44-50-56}, K2.

Rnd 12: K2, P7{9-12-14}, work C10F, P9{11-11-13}, work C10B, P7{9-12-14}, K4, P 38{44-50-56}, K2.

Rnds 13-65: Repeat Rnds 1-12, 4 times; then repeat Rnds 1-5 once **more**.

FRONT

Row 1 (Right side)**:** With straight knitting needles, K2, P7{9-12-14}, K4, P2, K4, P9{11-11-13}, K4, P2, K4, P7{9-12-14}, K2, leave remaining sts unworked on circular knitting needle (Back): 47{53-59-65} sts.

Row 2: P2, K7{9-12-14}, P4, K2, P4, K9{11-11-13}, P4, K2, P4, K7{9-12-14}, P2.

Row 3: K2, P7{9-12-14}, K4, P2, K4, P9{11-11-13}, K4, P2, K4, P7{9-12-14}, K2.

Rows 4-6: Repeat Rows 2 and 3 once, then repeat Row 2 once **more**.

Row 7: K2, P7{9-12-14}, work C10F, P9{11-11-13}, work C10B, P7{9-12-14}, K2.

Row 8: P2, K7{9-12-14}, P4, K2, P4, K9{11-11-13}, P4, K2, P4, K7{9-12-14}, P2.

Row 9: K2, P7{9-12-14}, K4, P2, K4, P9{11-11-13}, K4, P2, K4, P7{9-12-14}, K2.

Rows 10-18: Repeat Rows 8 and 9, 4 times; then repeat Row 8 once **more**.

Repeat Rows 7-18 for pattern until Front measures approximately 7{7½-8-8½}"/18{19-20.5-21.5} cm, ending by working a **wrong** side row.

Last Row: Slip first 8{10-13-15} sts onto a st holder (left shoulder); bind off center 31{33-33-35} sts **loosely** in **knit**; slip remaining 8{10-13-15} sts onto a second st holder (right shoulder).

BACK

Row 1: With **right** side facing, using straight knitting needles, and working across sts on circular knitting needle, K2, P 38{44-50-56}, K2: 42{48-54-60} sts.

Row 2: P2, K 38{44-50-56}, P2.

Row 3: K2, P 38{44-50-56}, P2.

Repeat Rows 2 and 3 for pattern until Back measures same as Front, ending by working a **wrong** side row.

Last Row: Slip first 8{10-13-15} sts onto a st holder (right shoulder); bind off center 26{28-28-30} sts **loosely** in **knit**; slip remaining 8{10-13-15} sts onto a second st holder (left shoulder).

Slip sts from Front and Back right shoulder st holders onto double-pointed knitting needles. Work 3-Needle Bind off *(Fig. 8, page 93)*.

Repeat for left shoulder.

RIGHT SLEEVE
BODY

With **right** side facing, using double-pointed knitting needles, and beginning at underarm, pick up 22{24-25-27} sts to shoulder *(Fig. 9a, page 93)*, pick up 22{24-25-27} sts to underarm; place a marker to mark the beginning of the rnd: 44{48-50-54} sts.

Rnds 1-11: K2, P 15{17-18-20}, K4, P2, K4, P 15{17-18-20}, K2.

Rnd 12: K2, P2 tog *(Fig. 4, page 92)*, P 13{15-16-18}, work C10F, P 13{15-16-18}, P2 tog, K2: 42{46-48-52} sts.

Rnds 13-19: K2, P 14{16-17-19}, K4, P2, K4, P 14{16-17-19}, K2.

Instructions continued on page 62.

Rnd 20 (Decrease row)**:** K2, P2 tog, P 12{14-15-17}, K4, P2, K4, P 12{14-15-17}, P2 tog, K2: 40{44-46-50} sts.

Rnds 21-23: K2, P 13{15-16-18}, K4, P2, K4, P 13{15-16-18}, K2.

Rnd 24: K2, P 13{15-16-18}, work C10F, P 13{15-16-18}, K2.

Rnds 25-27: K2, P 13{15-16-18}, K4, P2, K4, P 13{15-16-18}, K2.

Rnd 28 (Decrease row)**:** K2, P2 tog, P 11{13-14-16}, K4, P2, K4, P 11{13-14-16}, P2 tog, K2: 38{42-44-48} sts.

Continue in established pattern decreasing two purl sts in same manner, every 8th row, 3{3-2-3} times **more**; then decrease every 6th row, 0{0-2-1} time(s) *(see Zeros, page 92)*: 32{36-36-40} sts.

Work even until Sleeve measures approximately 14{14½-15-15½}"/35.5{37-38-39.5} cm.

RIBBING
Rnd 1: K1, P2, (K2, P2) around to last st, K1.

Repeat Rnd 1 until Sleeve measures approximately 16½{17-17½-18}"/42{43-44.5-45.5} cm.

Bind off all sts **loosely** in **knit**.

LEFT SLEEVE
BODY
With **right** side facing, using double-pointed knitting needles, and beginning at underarm, pick up 22{24-25-27} sts to shoulder, pick up 22{24-25-27} sts to underarm; place a marker to mark the beginning of the rnd: 44{48-50-54} sts.

Rnds 1-11: K2, P 15{17-18-20}, K4, P2, K4, P 15{17-18-20}, K2.

Rnd 12: K2, P2 tog, P 13{15-16-18}, work C10B, P 13{15-16-18}, P2 tog, K2: 42{46-48-52} sts.

Rnds 13-19: K2, P 14{16-17-19}, K4, P2, K4, P 14{16-17-19}, K2.

Rnd 20 (Decrease row)**:** K2, P2 tog, P 12{14-15-17}, K4, P2, K4, P 12{14-15-17}, P2 tog, K2: 40{44-46-50} sts.

Rnds 21-23: K2, P 13{15-16-18}, K4, P2, K4, P 13{15-16-18}, K2.

Rnd 24: K2, P 13{15-16-18}, work C10B, P 13{15-16-18}, K2.

Rnds 25-27: K2, P 13{15-16-18}, K4, P2, K4, P 13{15-16-18}, K2.

Rnd 28 (Decrease row)**:** K2, P2 tog, P 11{13-14-16}, K4, P2, K4, P 11{13-14-16}, P2 tog, K2: 38{42-44-48} sts.

Continue in established pattern decreasing two purl sts in same manner, every 8th row, 3{3-2-3} times **more**; then decrease every 6th row, 0{0-2-1} time(s): 32{36-36-40} sts.

Work even until Sleeve measures approximately 14{14½-15-15½}"/35.5{37-38-39.5} cm.

RIBBING
Rnd 1: K1, P2, (K2, P2) around to last st, K1.

Repeat Rnd 1 until Sleeve measures approximately 16½{17-17½-18}"/42{43-44.5-45.5} cm.

Bind off all sts **loosely** in **knit**.

FINISHING
See Crochet Stitches, page 94.

NECK EDGING
Rnd 1: With **right** side facing and using the crochet hook, join yarn with sc in any shoulder seam *(see Joining With Sc, page 94)*; sc in back loop only of each st across to next shoulder seam, sc in shoulder seam, sc in back loop only of each st across; join with slip st to **both** loops of first sc: 59{63-63-67} sc.

Rnd 2: Ch 1, sc in Back Loop Only *(Fig. 16, page 94)* of same st and each sc around; join with slip st to **both** loops of first sc, finish off.

BOTTOM EDGING

Rnd 1: With **right** side of cast on edge facing and using the crochet hook, join yarn with sc in back loop only of any st; sc in back loop only of each st around; join with slip st to **both** loops of first sc: 89{101-113-125} sts.

Rnd 2: Ch 1, sc in Back Loop Only of same st and each sc around; join with slip st to **both** loops of first sc, finish off.

SLEEVE EDGING

Rnd 1: With **right** side facing and using the crochet hook, join yarn with sc in back loop only of any st; sc in back loop only of each st around; join with slip st to **both** loops of first sc: 32{36-36-40} sts.

Rnd 2: Ch 1, sc in Back Loop Only of same st and each sc around; join with slip st to **both** loops of first sc, finish off.

Repeat around second Sleeve.

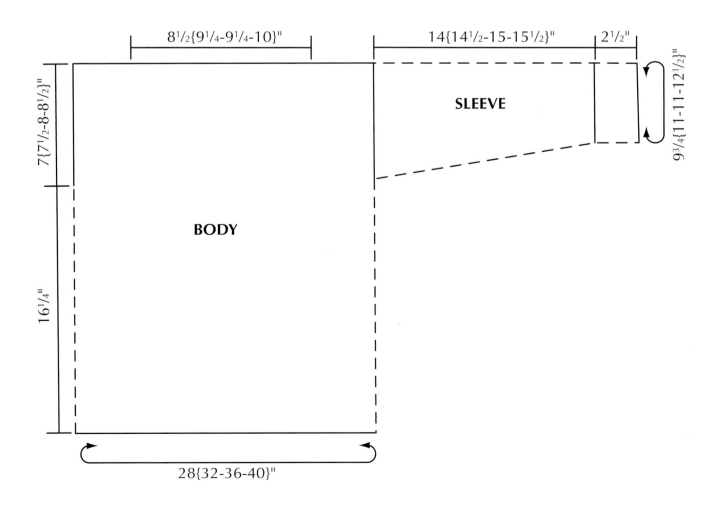

BODY

SLEEVE

8¹/₂{9¹/₄-9¹/₄-10}"

14{14¹/₂-15-15¹/₂}"

2¹/₂"

7{7¹/₂-8-8¹/₂}"

9³/₄{11-11-12¹/₂}"

16¹/₄"

28{32-36-40}"

Note: Dashed lines indicate continuous rounds.

Turtleneck Dress

Shown on pages 64 and 65.

⬤⬤⬤◼▷ EXPERIENCED

Size	Finished Chest Measurement
X-Small	30" (76 cm)
Small	33" (84 cm)
Medium	36" (91.5 cm)
Large	40" (101.5 cm)

Size Note: Instructions are written for size X-Small with sizes Small, Medium and Large in braces { }. Instructions will be easier to read if you circle all the numbers pertaining to your size. If only one number is given, it applies to all sizes.

MATERIALS

Bulky Weight Yarn
[3.5 ounces, 148 yards
(100 grams, 136 meters) per skein]:
    8{9-10-11} skeins
29" (73.5 cm) Circular knitting needle,
    size 11 (8 mm) **or** size needed for gauge
Straight knitting needles, size 11 (8 mm)
Double-pointed knitting needles, size 11 (8 mm)
Markers
Cable needle
Stitch holders - 6
Yarn needle

GAUGE: In pattern (slightly stretched),
16 sts and 16 rnds/rows = 4" (10 cm)

STITCH GUIDE

CABLE 4 BACK *(abbreviated C4B)*
    (uses next 4 sts)
Slip next 2 sts onto cable needle and hold at **back** of work, K2 from left needle, P2 from cable needle.

CABLE 4 FRONT *(abbreviated C4F)*
    (uses next 4 sts)
Slip next 2 sts onto cable needle and hold at **front** of work, P2 from left needle, K2 from cable needle.

CABLE 6 FRONT *(abbreviated C6F)*
    (uses next 6 sts)
Slip next 4 sts onto cable needle and hold at **front** of work, K2 from left needle, slip last 2 sts from cable needle **back** onto left needle and knit them, K2 from cable needle.

Body is worked in one piece to underarm.

BODY

With circular knitting needle, cast on 120{132-146-158} sts; place a marker to mark the beginning of the rnd (see **Knitting in the Round and Markers, pages 91 and 92**).

Rnd 1 (Right side)**:** P1{2-4-5}, K2, (P2, K2) twice, † P2{3-4-5}, K2, (P2, K2) twice †; repeat from † to † 3 times **more**, P1{2-4-5}, place a marker for side, P1{2-4-5}, K2, (P2, K2) twice, repeat from † to † 4 times, P1{2-4-5}.

Rnds 2-7: P1{2-4-5}, K2, (P2, K2) twice, † P2{3-4-5}, K2, (P2, K2) twice †; repeat from † to † 3 times **more**, P2{4-8-10}, K2, (P2, K2) twice, repeat from † to † 4 times, P1{2-4-5}.

Rnd 8: P1{2-4-5}, C4F, K2, C4B, † P2{3-4-5}, K2, (P2, K2) twice, P2{3-4-5}, C4F, K2, C4B †; repeat from † to † once **more**, P2{4-8-10}, K2, (P2, K2) twice, P2{3-4-5}, C4F, K2, C4B, repeat from † to † once, P2{3-4-5}, K2, (P2, K2) twice, P1{2-4-5}.

Rnd 9: P3{4-6-7}, K6, † P4{5-6-7}, K2, (P2, K2) twice, P4{5-6-7}, K6 †; repeat from † to † once **more**, P4{6-10-12}, K2, (P2, K2) twice, P4{5-6-7}, K6, repeat from † to † once, P4{5-6-7}, K2, (P2, K2) twice, P1{2-4-5}.

Rnd 10: P3{4-6-7}, C6F, † P4{5-6-7}, K2, (P2, K2) twice, P4{5-6-7}, C6F †; repeat from † to † once **more**, P4{6-10-12}, K2, (P2, K2) twice, P4{5-6-7}, C6F, repeat from † to † once, P4{5-6-7}, K2, (P2, K2) twice, P1{2-4-5}.

Rnd 11: Repeat Rnd 9.

Rnd 12: P1{2-4-5}, C4B, K2, C4F, † P2{3-4-5}, K2, (P2, K2) twice, P2{3-4-5}, C4B, K2, C4F †; repeat from † to † once **more**, P2{4-8-10}, K2, (P2, K2) twice, P2{3-4-5}, C4B, K2, C4F, repeat from † to † once, P2{3-4-5}, K2, (P2, K2) twice, P1{2-4-5}.

Rnd 13: P1{2-4-5}, K2, (P2, K2) twice, † P2{3-4-5}, K2, (P2, K2) twice †; repeat from † to † 3 times **more**, P2{4-8-10}, K2, (P2, K2) twice, repeat from † to † 4 times, P1{2-4-5}.

Rnd 14: P1{2-4-5}, K2, (P2, K2) twice, † P2{3-4-5}, C4F, K2, C4B, P2{3-4-5}, K2, (P2, K2) twice †; repeat from † to † once **more**, P2{4-8-10}, C4F, K2, C4B, P2{3-4-5}, K2, (P2, K2) twice, repeat from † to † once, P2{3-4-5}, C4F, K2, C4B, P1{2-4-5}.

Rnd 15: P1{2-4-5}, K2, (P2, K2) twice, † P4{5-6-7}, K6, P4{5-6-7}, K2, (P2, K2) twice †; repeat from † to † once **more**, P4{6-10-12}, K6, P4{5-6-7}, K2, (P2, K2) twice, repeat from † to † once, P4{5-6-7}, K6, P3{5-6-7}.

Rnd 16: P1{2-4-5}, K2, (P2, K2) twice, † P4{5-6-7}, C6F, P4{5-6-7}, K2, (P2, K2) twice †; repeat from † to † once **more**, P4{6-10-12}, C6F, P4{5-6-7}, K2, (P2, K2) twice, repeat from † to † once, P4{5-6-7}, C6F, P3{5-6-7}.

Rnd 17: Repeat Rnd 15.

Rnd 18: P1{2-4-5}, K2, (P2, K2) twice, † P2{3-4-5}, C4B, K2, C4F, P2{3-4-5}, K2, (P2, K2) twice †; repeat from † to † once **more**, P2{4-8-10}, C4B, K2, C4F, P2{3-4-5}, K2, (P2, K2) twice, repeat from † to † once, P2{3-4-5}, C4B, K2, C4F, P1{2-4-5}.

Rnd 19: Repeat Rnd 13.

Repeat Rnds 8-19 for pattern until Body measures approximately 36" (91.5 cm) from cast on edge **or desired length to underarm**, ending by working Rnd 5 or Rnd 17.

FRONT

Row 1 (Right side)**:** With straight knitting needles, P1{2-4-5}, K2, (P2, K2) twice, ★ P2{3-4-5}, K2, (P2, K2) twice; repeat from ★ 3 times **more**, P1{2-4-5}, leave remaining sts unworked on circular knitting needle (Back): 60{66-74-80} sts.

Instructions continued on page 68.

Row 2: K1{2-4-5}, P2, (K2, P2) twice,
★ K2{3-4-5}, P2, (K2, P2) twice; repeat from ★
3 times **more**, K1{2-4-5}.

Row 3: P1{2-4-5}, C4F, K2, C4B, ★ P2{3-4-5}, K2,
(P2, K2) twice, P2{3-4-5}, C4F, K2, C4B; repeat from
★ once **more**, K1{2-4-5}.

Row 4: K3{4-6-7}, P6, ★ K4{5-6-7}, P2, (K2, P2)
twice, K4{5-6-7}, P6; repeat from ★ once **more**,
K3{4-6-7}.

Row 5: P3{4-6-7}, C6F, ★ P4{5-6-7}, K2, (P2, K2)
twice, P4{5-6-7}, C6F; repeat from ★ once **more**,
P3{4-6-7}.

Row 6: Repeat Row 4.

Row 7: P1{2-4-5}, C4B, K2, C4F, ★ P2{3-4-5}, K2,
(P2, K2) twice, P2{3-4-5}, C4B, K2, C4F; repeat
from ★ once **more**, K1{2-4-5}.

Row 8: Repeat Row 2.

Row 9: P1{2-4-5}, K2, (P2, K2) twice, ★ P2{3-4-5},
C4F, K2, C4B, P2{3-4-5}, K2, (P2, K2) twice; repeat
from ★ once **more**, P1{2-4-5}.

Row 10: K1{2-4-5}, P2, (K2, P2) twice,
★ K4{5-6-7}, P6, K4{5-6-7}, P2, (K2, P2) twice;
repeat from ★ once **more**, K1{2-4-5}.

Row 11: P1{2-4-5}, K2, (P2, K2) twice,
★ P4{5-6-7}, C6F, P4{5-6-7}, K2, (P2, K2) twice;
repeat from ★ once **more**, P1{2-4-5}.

Row 12: Repeat Row 10.

Row 13: P1{2-4-5}, K2, (P2, K2) twice,
★ P2{3-4-5}, C4B, K2, C4F, P2{3-4-5}, K2,
(P2, K2) twice; repeat from ★ once **more**, P1{2-4-5}.

Repeat Rows 2-13 for pattern until Front measures
approximately 6¹/₂{7-7¹/₂-8}"/16.5{18-19-20.5} cm,
ending by working a **wrong** side row.

SHOULDER SHAPING

Maintain established pattern throughout.

Row 1: Work across 14{16-20-22} sts, slip sts just
worked onto a st holder, work across.

Row 2: Work across 14{16-20-22} sts, slip sts just
worked onto st holder, P1{1-0-0} **(see Zeros,
page 92)**, (K2, P2) twice, K2{3-4-5}, work across,
slip 32{34-33-35} sts just worked onto a st holder
(neck); cut yarn.

Make a note of the last Cable Pattern Row worked
to continue in established Cable Pattern on center
10 sts of Turtleneck.

BACK

Row 1: With **right** side facing, using straight
knitting needles, and working across sts on circular
knitting needle, P1{2-4-5}, K2, (P2, K2) twice,
★ P2{3-4-5}, K2, (P2, K2) twice; repeat from ★
3 times **more**, P1{2-4-5}.

Beginning with Row 2, complete same as Front.

Slip sts from Front and Back right shoulder
st holders onto double-pointed knitting needles.
Work 3-Needle Bind off **(Fig. 8, page 93)**.

Repeat for left shoulder.

FINISHING
TURTLENECK

With **right** side facing, slip 32{34-33-35} sts
from Front st holder and Back st holder onto
double-pointed knitting needles, dividing sts evenly,
place a marker to mark the beginning of the rnd:
64{68-66-70} sts.

Rnds 1-9: Maintain established Cable Pattern on
center 10 sts of Front and Back and ribbing pattern
on each side.

Bind off all sts **loosely** in pattern.

SLEEVE
BODY
With **right** side facing, beginning at underarm, and using double-pointed knitting needles, pick up 52{56-60-64} sts evenly spaced around *(Figs. 9a & b, page 93)*, place a marker to mark the beginning of the rnd.

Rnds 1-7: P5{7-7-7}, K2, P2{2-3-4}, K2, ★ (P2, K2) twice, P2{2-3-4}, K2; repeat from ★ 2 times **more**, P5{7-7-7}.

Rnd 8: P5{7-7-7}, K2, † P2{2-3-4}, C4F, K2, C4B, P2{2-3-4}, K2 †, (P2, K2) twice, repeat from † to † once, P5{7-7-7}.

Rnd 9 (Decrease rnd)**:** P1, P2 tog *(Fig. 4, page 92)*, P2{4-4-4}, K2, P4{4-5-6}, K6, P4{4-5-6}, K2, (P2, K2) twice, P4{5-6-7}, K6, P4{5-6-7}, K2, P2{4-4-4}, P2 tog, P1: 50{54-58-62} sts.

Rnd 10: P4{6-6-6}, K2, P4{4-5-6}, C6F, P4{4-5-6}, K2, (P2, K2) twice, P4{5-6-7}, C6F, P4{5-6-7}, K2, P4{6-6-6}.

Rnd 11: P4{6-6-6}, K2, P4{4-5-6}, K6, P4{4-5-6}, K2, (P2, K2) twice, P4{5-6-7}, K6, P4{5-6-7}, K2, P4{6-6-6}.

Rnd 12: P4{6-6-6}, K2, † P2{2-3-4}, C4B, K2, C4F, P2{2-3-4}, K2 †, (P2, K2) twice, repeat from † to † once, P4{6-6-6}.

Rnd 13 (Decrease rnd)**:** P1, P2 tog, P1{3-3-3}, K2, P2{2-3-4}, K2, ★ (P2, K2) twice, P2{2-3-4}, K2; repeat from ★ 2 times **more**, P1{3-3-3}, P2 tog, P1: 48{52-56-60} sts.

Rnd 14: P3{5-5-5}, K2, P2{2-3-4}, K2, (P2, K2) twice, P2{2-3-4}, C4F, K2, C4B, P2{2-3-4}, K2, (P2, K2) twice, P2{2-3-4}, K2, P3{5-5-5}.

Rnd 15: P3{5-5-5}, K2, P2{2-3-4}, K2, (P2, K2) twice, P4{4-5-6}, K6, P4{4-5-6}, K2, (P2, K2) twice, P2{2-3-4}, K2, P3{5-5-5}.

Rnd 16: P3{5-5-5}, K2, P2{2-3-4}, K2, (P2, K2) twice, P4{4-5-6}, C6F, P4{4-5-6}, K2, (P2, K2) twice, P2{2-3-4}, K2, P3{5-5-5}.

Rnd 17 (Decrease rnd)**:** P1, P2 tog, P 0{2-2-2}, K2, P2{2-3-4}, K2, (P2, K2) twice, P4{4-5-6}, K6, P4{4-5-6}, K2, (P2, K2) twice, P2{2-3-4}, K2, P 0{2-2-2}, P2 tog, P1: 46{50-54-58} sts.

Rnd 18: P2{4-4-4}, K2, P2{2-3-4}, K2, (P2, K2) twice, P2{2-3-4}, C4F, K2, C4B, P2{2-3-4}, K2, (P2, K2) twice, P2{2-3-4}, K2, P2{4-4-4}.

Rnd 19: P2{4-4-4}, K2, P2{2-3-4}, K2, ★ (P2, K2) twice, P2{2-3-4}, K2; repeat from ★ 2 times **more**, P2{4-4-4}.

Maintaining established pattern (Rnds 8-19), continue to decrease in same manner, every fourth rnd, 4{6-6-6} times **more**; then decrease every other rnd, 3{1-3-3} time(s): 32{36-36-40} sts.

Work even until Sleeve measures approximately 13{14-15-16}"/33{35.5-38-40.5} cm.

RIBBING
Work in K2, P2 ribbing around for 2½" (6.5 cm).

Bind off all sts **loosely** in ribbing.

Repeat for second Sleeve.

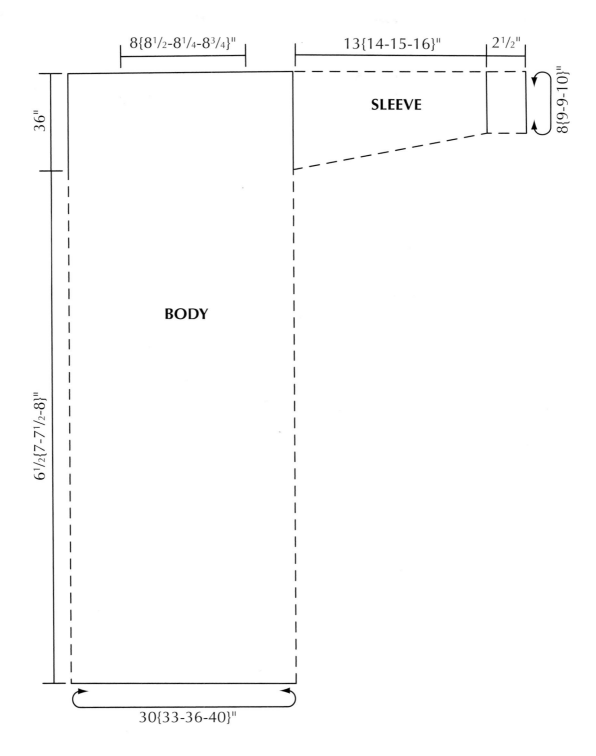

8{8½-8¼-8¾}" 13{14-15-16}" 2½"

36"

8{9-9-10}"

SLEEVE

BODY

6½{7-7½-8}"

30{33-36-40}"

Note: Dashed lines indicate continuous rounds.

Skirt

Shown on pages 72 and 73.

◖◼◼◻ **INTERMEDIATE**

Size	Finished Hip Measurement
X-Small	28³/₄" (73 cm)
Small	34¹/₂" (87.5 cm)
Medium	40¹/₄" (102 cm)
Large	46" (117 cm)

Size Note: Instructions are written for size X-Small with sizes Small, Medium, and Large in braces { }. Instructions will be easier to read if you circle all the numbers pertaining to your size. If only one number is given, it applies to all sizes.

MATERIALS

Light Weight Yarn
[3.52 ounces, 218 yards
(100 grams, 200 meters) per skein]:
  7{8-9-10} skeins
29" (73.5 cm) Circular knitting needle,
  size 8 (5 mm) **or** size needed for gauge
Cable needle
Marker
Crochet hook, size H (5 mm)

GAUGE: With two strands of yarn held together, in pattern (slightly stretched), 28 sts = 5³/₄" (14.5 cm); 25 rows = 4" (10 cm)

STITCH GUIDE

CABLE 6 FRONT (abbreviated C6F)
  (uses next 6 sts)
Slip next 4 sts onto cable needle and hold at **front** of work, K2 from left needle, slip last 2 sts from cable needle **back** to left needle and purl them, then K2 from cable needle.

CABLE 6 BACK (abbreviated C6B)
  (uses next 6 sts)
Slip next 4 sts onto cable needle and hold at **back** of work, K2 from left needle, slip last 2 sts from cable needle **back** to left needle and purl them, then K2 from cable needle.

CABLE 6 FRONT KNIT (abbreviated C6FK)
  (uses next 6 sts)
Slip next 4 sts onto cable needle and hold at **front** of work, K2 from left needle, slip last 2 sts from cable needle **back** to left needle and knit them, then K2 from cable needle.

CABLE 6 BACK KNIT (abbreviated C6BK)
  (uses next 6 sts)
Slip next 4 sts onto cable needle and hold at **back** of work, K2 from left needle, slip last 2 sts from cable needle **back** to left needle and knit them, then K2 from cable needle.

CABLE 4 FRONT *(abbreviated C4F)*
  (uses next 4 sts)
Slip next 2 sts onto cable needle and hold at **front** of work, P2 from left needle, then K2 from cable needle.

CABLE 4 BACK *(abbreviated C4B)*
  (uses next 4 sts)
Slip next 2 sts onto cable needle and hold at **back** of work, K2 from left needle, then P2 from cable needle.

Skirt is worked as a tube and measures approximately 24" (61 cm) long after turning down waist casing. The length of Skirt may be made longer or shorter as desired, by changing the number of times Rnds 31-38 or Rnds 65-74 are repeated. Yarn requirements should be adjusted accordingly.

SKIRT

With two strands of yarn held together, cast on 140{168-196-224} sts; place a marker to mark the beginning of the rnd *(see Knitting in the Round and Markers, pages 91 and 92)*.

Rnds 1-6: (P2, K2) around.

Rnd 7: P2, K2, P2, C6F, ★ P2, (K2, P2) 5 times, C6F; repeat from ★ around to last 16 sts, (P2, K2) 4 times.

Rnds 8-10: (P2, K2) around.

Rnd 11: ★ P2, C6F, P2, C6B, P2, C4F, K2, C4B; repeat from ★ around.

Rnds 12-14: Knit the knit sts and purl the purl sts as they face you.

Rnd 15: ★ P2, K2, P2, C6F, P2, K2, P2, C4B, K2, C4F; repeat from ★ around.

Rnds 16-23: Repeat Rnds 8-15.

Rnds 24-30: (P2, K2) around.

Rnd 31: ★ P2, K2, (P2, C6F, P2, K2) twice; repeat from ★ around.

Rnds 32-34: (P2, K2) around.

Rnd 35: P2, (K2, P2) 4 times, C6B, ★ P2, (K2, P2) 5 times, C6B; repeat from ★ around to last 4 sts, P2, K2.

Rnds 36-38: (P2, K2) around.

Rnds 39-59: Repeat Rnds 31-38 twice, then repeat Rnds 31-35 once **more**.

Rnds 60-65: (P2, K2) around.

Row 66: (P2, K2) around to last 4 sts, place marker **before** these last 4 sts to mark beginning of Rnd 67.

Rnd 67: ★ P2, (C4F, K2, C4B, P2) twice, K2; repeat from ★ around.

Rnd 68: Knit the knit sts and purl the purl sts as they face you.

Rnd 69: (P4, C6FK, P6, C6FK, P4, K2) around.

Rnd 70: Knit the knit sts and purl the purl sts as they face you.

Rnd 71: ★ P2, (C4B, K2, C4F, P2) twice, K2; repeat from ★ around.

Rnds 72-76: (P2, K2) around.

Rnds 77-105: Repeat Rnds 67-76 twice, then repeat Rnds 67-75 once **more**.

Rnd 106: Remove the beginning of the rnd marker, (P2, K2) twice, place a marker after working these 8 sts to mark the beginning of Rnd 106; (P2, K2) around.

Rnd 107: ★ P2, C6B, P2, K2, P2, C4F, K2, C4B, P2, K2; repeat from ★ around.

Rnd 108: Knit the knit sts and purl the purl sts as they face you.

Instructions continued on page 77.

Rnd 109: ★ (P2, K2) 3 times, P4, C6BK, P4, K2; repeat from ★ around.

Rnd 110: Knit the knit sts and purl the purl sts as they face you.

Rnd 111: P2, (K2, P2) 3 times, C4B, K2, C4F, P2, ★ (K2, P2) 4 times, C4B, K2, C4F, P2; repeat from ★ around to last 2 sts, K2.

Rnds 112-114: (P2, K2) around.

Rnd 115: P2, C6B, P2, C6F, P2, K2, P2, ★ (C6B, P2) twice, C6F, P2, K2, P2; repeat from ★ around to last 6 sts, C6B.

Rnds 116-122: (P2, K2) around.

Rnd 123: ★ P2, C6B, P2, K2, P2, C4F, K2, C4B, P2, K2; repeat from ★ around.

Rnds 124-126: Knit the knit sts and purl the purl sts as they face you.

Rnd 127: P2, (K2, P2) 3 times, C4B, K2, C4F, P2, ★ (K2, P2) 4 times, C4B, K2, C4F, P2; repeat from ★ around to last 2 sts, K2.

Rnds 128-130: (P2, K2) around.

Rnd 131: ★ P2, C6B, (P2, K2) 5 times; repeat from ★ around.

Rnds 132-134: (P2, K2) around.

Rnd 135: P2, (K2, P2) 3 times, C4F, K2, C4B, P2, ★ (K2, P2) 4 times, C4F, K2, C4B, P2; repeat from ★ around to last 2 sts, K2.

Rnds 136-138: Knit the knit sts and purl the purl sts as they face you.

Rnd 139: P2, (K2, P2) 3 times, C4B, K2, C4F, P2, ★ (K2, P2) 4 times, C4B, K2, C4F, P2; repeat from ★ around to last 2 sts, K2.

Rnds 140-145: (P2, K2) around.

Bind off all sts in **knit**.

FINISHING

Fold bound-off edge of Skirt ½" (12 mm) to **wrong** side to form a casing and pin in place.

See Crochet Stitches, page 94.

Using the crochet hook, and working in back loops only of every other bound-off stitch **and** in a stitch from skirt, join single strand of yarn with sc at center front *(see **Joining With Sc, page 94**)*; sc around edge but do **not** join to first sc at end of round; finish off leaving a space between the first and the last sc.

With two strands of yarn held together, crochet a chain long enough to go around the waist plus 16" (40.5 cm) then finish off.

Run the chain through the waist casing, entering the casing between the beginning and ending sc sts.

Tie a knot in each end of the chain and cut the yarn strands, leaving tails 2" (5 cm) long.

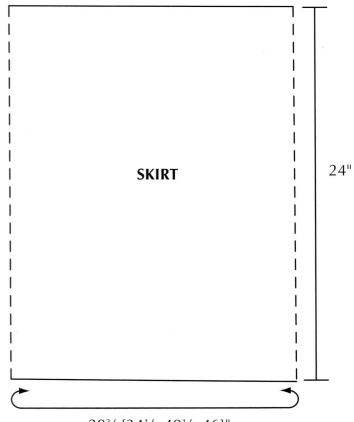

SKIRT

24"

28¾{34½-40¼-46}"

Note: Dashed lines indicate continuous rounds.

V-Neck Top

Shown on pages 78 and 79.

■■■□ INTERMEDIATE

Size	Finished Chest Measurement
X-Small	30" (76 cm)
Small	34" (86.5 cm)
Medium	38" (96.5 cm)
Large	42" (106.5 cm)

Size Note: Instructions are written for size X-Small with sizes Small, Medium and Large in braces { }. Instructions will be easier to read if you circle all the numbers pertaining to your size. If only one number is given, it applies to all sizes.

MATERIALS

Bulky Weight Yarn
[3 ounces, 135 yards,
(85 grams, 123 meters) per skein]:
   3{4-5-5} skeins
29" (73.5 cm) Circular knitting needle,
   size 11 (8 mm) **or** size needed for gauge
Straight knitting needles, size 11 (8 mm)
Double-pointed knitting needles, size 11 (8 mm)
Cable needle
Stitch holders - 4
Markers
Crochet hook, size J (6 mm)

GAUGE: In Stockinette Stitch,
   12 sts and 18 rows/rnds = 4" (10 cm)
   In pattern (slightly stretched),
   3 cables (18 sts) = 5" (12.75 cm)

STITCH GUIDE

FRONT CABLE *(abbreviated FC)*
   (uses next 6 sts)
Slip next 3 sts onto cable needle and hold at **front** of work, K3 from left needle, then K3 from cable needle.

BACK CABLE *(abbreviated BC)*
   (uses next 6 sts)
Slip next 3 sts onto cable needle and hold at **back** of work, K3 from left needle, then K3 from cable needle.

Body is made in one piece to the underarm.

BODY

With circular knitting needle, cast on 96{108-120-132} sts; place a marker to mark the beginning of the rnd *(see Knitting in the Round and Markers, pages 91 and 92)*.

Rnd 1 (Right side)**:** K 48{54-60-66}, place a marker to mark side, knit around.

Rnds 2 and 3: Knit around.

Rnd 4: K 11{13-15-17}, work FC, K 14{16-18-20}, work BC, knit around to next marker, slip marker, K 15{18-21-24}, work FC 3 times, knit around.

Rnds 5-7: Knit around.

Rnd 8: K8{10-12-14}, work BC twice, K8{10-12-14}, work FC twice, knit around to next marker, slip marker, K 12{15-18-21}, work BC 3 times, knit around.

Rnds 9-11: Knit around.

Rnds 12-19: Repeat Rnds 4-11.

Rnd 20: K8{10-12-14}, work BC twice, K8{10-12-14}, work FC twice, knit around to next marker, slip marker, K9{12-15-18}, work FC 5 times, knit around.

Rnds 21-23: Knit around.

Rnd 24: K 11{13-15-17}, work FC, K 14{16-18-20}, work BC, knit around to next marker, slip marker, K6{9-12-15}, work BC 6 times, knit around.

Rnds 25-27: Knit around.

Rnds 28-35: Repeat Rnds 20-27.

Rnd 36: K8{10-12-14}, work BC twice, K8{10-12-14}, work FC twice, knit around to next marker, slip marker, K3{6-9-12}, work FC 7 times, knit around.

Rnds 37-39: Knit around.

Rnd 40: K 11{13-15-17}, work FC, K 14{16-18-20}, work BC, knit around to next marker, slip marker, K6{9-12-15}, work BC 6 times, knit around.

Rnds 41-43: Knit around.

Rnds 44-47: Repeat Rnds 36-39.

Rnd 48: K 11{13-15-17}, work FC, K 14{16-18-20}, work BC, knit around to next marker, slip marker, K 0{3-6-9} *(see Zeros, page 92)*, work BC 8 times, K 0{3-6-9}.

Rnds 49-51: Knit around.

SIZES MEDIUM & LARGE ONLY
Rnd 52: K{12-14}, work BC twice, K{12-14}, work FC twice, knit around to next marker, slip marker, K{9-12}, work FC 7 times, knit around.

Rnds 53-55: Knit around.

Rnd 56: K {15-17}, work FC, K {18-20}, work BC, knit around to next marker, slip marker, K{6-9}, work BC 8 times, K{6-9}.

Rnds 57-59: Knit around.

BACK
Row 1 (Right side)**:** With straight knitting needles, K8{10-12-14}, work BC twice, K8{10-12-14}, work FC twice, K8{10-12-14}, leave remaining sts unworked on circular knitting needle (Front): 48{54-60-66} sts.

Row 2: Purl across.

Row 3: Knit across.

Row 4: Purl across.

Row 5: K 11{13-15-17}, work FC, K 14{16-18-20}, work BC, K 11{13-15-17}.

Row 6: Purl across.

Row 7: Knit across.

Row 8: Purl across.

Row 9: K8{10-12-14}, work BC twice, K8{10-12-14}, work FC twice, K8{10-12-14}.

Instructions continued on page 82.

Rows 10 thru 25{25-33-33}: Repeat Rows 2-9, 2{2-3-3} times.

Size X-Small ONLY - Rows 26 thru 30: Repeat Rows 2-6 once.

Size Small ONLY - Rows 26 thru 32: Repeat Rows 2-8 once.

Size Medium ONLY - Row 34: Purl across.

Size Large ONLY - Rows 34 thru 36: Repeat Rows 2-4 once.

All Sizes - Last Row: K 14{16-19-21}, slip sts just worked onto a st holder (right shoulder), bind off center 20{22-22-24} sts, knit across remaining sts, slip 14{16-19-21} sts just worked onto a second st holder (left shoulder).

LEFT FRONT
Row 1: With **right** side facing, using straight knitting needles, and working across sts on circular knitting needle, K3{6-9-12}, work FC 3 times, K3, slip remaining 24{27-30-33} sts onto a st holder (Right Front): 24{27-30-33} sts.

Row 2: Purl across.

Row 3: Knit across.

Row 4: Purl across.

Row 5: K 0{3-6-9}, work BC 4 times.

Row 6: Purl across.

Row 7 (Decrease row)**:** K1, SSK *(Figs. 5a-c, page 92)*, knit across: 23{26-29-32} sts.

Row 8: Purl across.

Row 9: K1, SSK, K5{2-5-8}, work FC 2{3-3-3} times, K3: 22{25-28-31} sts.

Rows 10-12: Repeat Rows 6-8: 21{24-27-30} sts.

Row 13: K1, SSK, work BC 3 times: 20{23-26-29} sts.

Rows 14-16: Repeat Rows 6-8: 19{22-25-28} sts.

Row 17: K1, SSK, K1{4-1-4}, work FC 2{2-3-3} times, K3: 18{21-24-27} sts.

Rows 18-20: Repeat Rows 6-8: 17{20-23-26} sts.

Row 21: K1, SSK, K2{5-8-11}, work BC twice: 16{19-22-25} sts.

Rows 22-24: Repeat Rows 6-8: 15{18-21-24} sts.

Row 25: K1, SSK, K3{0-3-6}, work FC 1{2-2-2} time(s), K3: 14{17-20-23} sts.

Size X-Small ONLY
Row 26: Purl across.

Row 27: Knit across.

Rows 28-30: Repeat Rows 26 and 27 once, then repeat Row 26 once **more**.

Slip remaining sts onto a st holder.

Size Small, Medium & Large ONLY
Rows 26-28: Repeat Rows 6-8: {16-19-21} sts.

Row 29: (K1, SSK) {0-0-1} time(s), K {10-13-13}, work BC: {16-19-20} sts.

Row 30: Purl across.

Row 31: Knit across.

Next {1-3-5} Rows: Repeat Rows 30 and 31, {0-1-2} time(s); then repeat Row 30 once **more**.

Slip remaining sts onto a st holder.

RIGHT FRONT
Row 1: Slip sts from Right Front st holder onto empty straight knitting needle; with **right** side facing and using straight knitting needles, K3, work FC 3 times, K3{6-9-12}: 24{27-30-33} sts.

Row 2: Purl across.

Row 3: Knit across.

Row 4: Purl across.

Row 5: Work BC 4 times, K 0{3-6-9}.

Row 6: Purl across.

Row 7 (Decrease row)**:** Knit across to last 3 sts, K2 tog *(Fig. 3, page 92)*, K1: 23{26-29-32} sts.

Row 8: Purl across.

Row 9: K3, work FC 2{3-3-3} times, K5{2-5-8}, K2 tog, K1: 22{25-28-31} sts.

Rows 10-12: Repeat Rows 6-8: 21{24-27-30} sts.

Row 13: Work BC 3 times, K 0{3-6-9}, K2 tog, K1: 20{23-26-29} sts.

Rows 14-16: Repeat Rows 6-8: 19{22-25-28} sts.

Row 17: K3, work FC 2{2-3-3} times, K1{4-1-4}, K2 tog, K1: 18{21-24-27} sts.

Rows 18-20: Repeat Rows 6-8: 17{20-23-26} sts.

Row 21: Work BC twice, K2{5-8-11}, K2 tog, K1: 16{19-22-25} sts.

Rows 22-24: Repeat Rows 6-8: 15{18-21-24} sts.

Row 25: K3, work FC 1{2-2-2} time(s), K3{0-3-6}, K2 tog, K1: 14{17-20-23} sts.

Size X-Small ONLY
Row 26: Purl across.

Row 27: Knit across.

Rows 28-30: Repeat Rows 26 and 27 once, then repeat Row 26 once **more**.

Slip remaining sts onto a st holder.

Size Small, Medium & Large ONLY
Rows 26-28: Repeat Rows 6-8: {16-19-22} sts.

Row 29: Work BC, K {10-13-13}, (K2 tog, K1) {0-0-1} time(s).

Row 30: Purl across.

Row 31: Knit across.

Next {1-3-5} Rows: Repeat Rows 30 and 31, {0-1-2} time(s); then repeat Row 30 once **more**.

Slip remaining sts onto a st holder.

Slip sts from Front and Back right shoulder st holders onto double-pointed knitting needles. Work 3-Needle Bind off *(Fig. 8, page 93)*.

Repeat for left shoulder.

Instructions continued on page 85.

FINISHING

See Crochet Stitches, page 94.

NECK EDGING

Rnd 1: With **right** side facing and using the crochet hook, join yarn with sc in left shoulder seam *(see Joining With Sc, page 94)*; sc evenly across to center of "V", sc in "V", sc evenly across to right shoulder seam, sc in right shoulder seam and in back loop only of each bound-off st across back neck edge; join with slip st to **both** loops of first sc.

Rnd 2: Ch 1, working in Back Loops Only *(Fig. 16, page 94)* sc in same st and each sc across to within onesc of center sc at "V", pull up a loop in next sc, skip next sc, pull up a loop in next sc, YO and draw through all 3 loops on hook, sc in each sc around; join with slip st to **both** loops of first sc, finish off.

BOTTOM EDGING

Rnd 1: With **right** side of cast on edge facing and using the crochet hook, join yarn with sc in back loop only of any st; sc in back loop only of each st around; join with slip st to **both** loops of first sc: 96{108-120-132} sts.

Note: Measurements do **not** include Crochet Edgings. Dashed lines indicated continuous rounds.

Rnds 2 and 3: Ch 1, sc in Back Loop Only of same st and each sc around; join with slip st to **both** loops of first sc.

Finish off.

ARMHOLE EDGING

Rnd 1: With **right** side facing and using the crochet hook, join yarn with sc at underarm; sc evenly around entire armhole opening; join with slip st to first sc.

Rnds 2 and 3: Ch 1, sc in Back Loop Only of same st and each sc around; join with slip st to **both** loops of first sc.

Finish off.

Repeat around second Armhole.

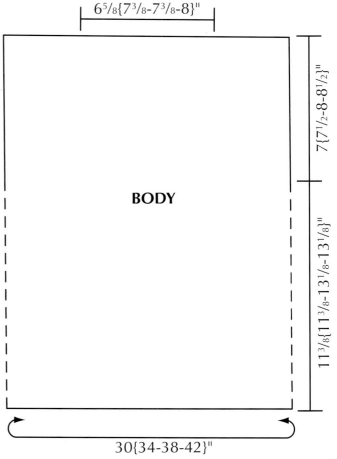

6⅝{7⅜-7⅜-8}"

7{7½-8-8½}"

11⅜{11⅜-13⅛-13⅛}"

BODY

30{34-38-42}"

Sleeveless Turtleneck

Shown on pages 86 and 87.

●■■■□ INTERMEDIATE

Size	Finished Chest Measurement
X-Small	27½" (70 cm)
Small	33" (84 cm)
Medium	38" (96.5 cm)
Large	43½" (110.5 cm)

Size Note: Instructions are written for size X-Small with sizes Small, Medium and Large in braces { }. Instructions will be easier to read if you circle all the numbers pertaining to your size. If only one number is given, it applies to all sizes.

MATERIALS

Super Bulky Weight Yarn
[6 ounces, 108 yards
(170 grams, 98 meters) per skein]:
   3{3-4-4} skeins
Straight knitting needles, size 13 (9 mm) **or**
   size needed for gauge
Cable needle
Stitch holders - 2
Crochet hook, size J (6 mm)
Yarn needle

GAUGE: In pattern (slightly stretched),
   16 sts = 5¼" (13.25 cm);
   14 rows/rnds = 4" (10 cm)

STITCH GUIDE

CABLE 6 FRONT *(abbreviated C6F)*
   (uses next 6 sts)
Slip next 4 sts onto cable needle and hold at **front** of work, K2 from left needle, slip last 2 sts from cable needle **back** to left needle and purl them, then K2 from cable needle.

CABLE 6 BACK *(abbreviated C6B)*
   (uses next 6 sts)
Slip next 4 sts onto cable needle and hold at **back** of work, K2 from left needle, slip last 2 sts from cable needle **back** to left needle and purl them, then K2 from cable needle.

BODY (Make 2)

Cast on 44{52-60-68} sts.

Row 1: K3, P2, (K2, P2) across to last 3 sts, K3.

Row 2 (Right side)**:** P3, K2, (P2, K2) across to last 3 sts, P3.

Rows 3-5: Repeat Rows 1 and 2 once, then repeat Row 1 once **more.**

Row 6: P3, C6F, (P2, C6F) across to last 3 sts, P3.

Row 7: K3, P2, (K2, P2) across to last 3 sts, K3.

Row 8: P3, K2, (P2, K2) across to last 3 sts, P3.

Rows 9-11: Repeat Rows 7 and 8 once, then repeat Row 7 once **more.**

Row 12: P3, K2, P2, (C6B, P2) across to last 5 sts, K2, P3.

Row 13: K3, P2, (K2, P2) across to last 3 sts, K3.

Row 14: P3, K2, (P2, K2) across to last 3 sts, P3.

Rows 15-17: Repeat Rows 13 and 14 once, then repeat Row 13 once **more**.

Row 18: P3, K2, P2, (C6B, P2) across to last 5 sts, K2, P3.

Repeat Rows 1-18 for pattern until Body measures approximately 20" (51 cm) from cast on edge **or desired length to shoulder**, ending by working Row 10.

Last Row: Bind off first 9{12-17-20} sts (shoulder), work across in pattern until you have 26{28-26-28} sts on the right needle, slip center 26{28-26-28} sts onto a st holder (neck), bind off remaining sts (shoulder).

FINISHING
Sew one shoulder seam.

TURTLENECK
SIZE X-SMALL & MEDIUM ONLY
Row 1: With **right** side facing and beginning at unsewn shoulder, slip 26 sts from first st holder onto empty knitting needle; † P2, K2, P2, (C6B, P2) twice, K2, P2 †; slip 26 sts from second st holder onto empty knitting needle, repeat from † to † once: 52 sts.

Row 2: (K2, P2) 6 times, K4, (P2, K2) across.

Row 3: (P2, K2) 6 times, P4, (K2, P2) across.

Rows 4-6: Repeat Rows 2 and 3 once, then repeat Row 2 once **more**.

Row 7: P2, K2, P2, (C6B, P2) twice, K2, P4, K2, P2, (C6B, P2) twice, K2, P2.

Rows 8-12: Repeat Rows 2-6.

Bind off all sts **loosely** in **knit**.

SIZE SMALL & LARGE ONLY
Row 1: With **right** side facing and beginning at unsewn shoulder, slip 28 sts from first st holder onto empty knitting needle; † K1, P2, (C6B, P2) 3 times, K1 †; slip 28 sts from second st holder onto empty knitting needle, repeat from † to † once: 56 sts.

Row 2: P1, K2, (P2, K2) across to last st, P1.

Row 3: K1, P2, (K2, P2) across to last st, K1.

Rows 4-6: Repeat Rows 2 and 3 once, then repeat Row 2 once **more**.

Row 7: K1, P2, (C6B, P2) 3 times, K2, P2, (C6B, P2) 3 times, K1.

Rows 8-12: Repeat Rows 2-6.

Bind off all sts **loosely** in **knit**.

Sew Turtleneck and shoulder in one continuous seam.

Sew side seams leaving a(n) 7{7$\frac{1}{2}$-8-8$\frac{1}{2}$}"/ 18{19-20.5-21.5} cm armhole opening.

EDGING
See Crochet Stitches, page 94.

NECK
With **right** side facing and using the crochet hook, join yarn with sc in seam *(see Joining With Sc, page 94)*; sc in back loop only of each st around; join with slip st to first sc, finish off.

ARMHOLE
With **right** side facing and using the crochet hook, join yarn with sc in underarm seam; sc evenly around armhole edge; join with slip st to first sc, finish off.

Repeat around second Armhole.

General Instructions

ABBREVIATIONS

BC	Back Cable
C3B	Cable 3 Back
C3F	Cable 3 Front
C4B	Cable 4 Back
C4F	Cable 4 Front
C5B	Cable 5 Back
C5F	Cable 5 Front
C6B	Cable 6 Back
C6BK	Cable 6 Back Knit
C6F	Cable 6 Front
C6FK	Cable 6 Front Knit
C7F	Cable 7 Front
C7B	Cable 7 Back
C9F	Cable 9 Front
C10B	Cable 10 Back
C10F	Cable 10 Front
ch(s)	chain(s)
cm	centimeters
FC	Front Cable
K	knit
mm	millimeters
P	purl
Rnd(s)	Round(s)
sc	single crochet(s)
SSK	slip, slip, knit
SSP	slip, slip, purl
st(s)	stitch(es)
tog	together
YO	yarn over

★ — work instructions following ★ as many **more** times as indicated in addition to the first time.

† to † — work all instructions from first † to second † **as many** times as specified.

( ) or [ ] — work enclosed instructions **as many** times as specified by the number immediately following **or** work all enclosed instructions from needle indicated **or** contains explanatory remarks.

colon (:) — the number(s) given after a colon at the end of a row or round denote(s) the number of stitches you should have on that row or round.

work even — work without increasing or decreasing in the established pattern.

KNIT TERMINOLOGY	
UNITED STATES	**INTERNATIONAL**
gauge =	tension
bind off =	cast off
yarn over (YO) =	yarn forward (yfwd) **or** yarn around needle (yrn)

Yarn Weight Symbol & Names	SUPER FINE 1	FINE 2	LIGHT 3	MEDIUM 4	BULKY 5	SUPER BULKY 6
Type of Yarns in Category	Sock, Fingering Baby	Sport, Baby	DK, Light Worsted	Worsted, Afghan, Aran	Chunky, Craft, Rug	Bulky, Roving
Crochet Gauge Ranges in Single Crochet to 4" (10 cm)	21-32 sts	16-20 sts	12-17 sts	11-14 sts	8-11 sts	5-9 sts
Advised Hook Size Range	B-1 to E-4	E-4 to 7	7 to I-9	I-9 to K-10.5	K-10.5 to M-13	M-13 and larger

CROCHET HOOKS												
U.S.	B-1	C-2	D-3	E-4	F-5	G-6	H-8	I-9	J-10	K-10½	N	P	Q
Metric - mm	2.25	2.75	3.25	3.5	3.75	4	5	5.5	6	6.5	9	10	15

KNITTING NEEDLES															
U.S.	0	1	2	3	4	5	6	7	8	9	10	10½	11	13	15	17
U.K.	13	12	11	10	9	8	7	6	5	4	3	2	1	00	000	---
Metric - mm	2	2.25	2.75	3.25	3.5	3.75	4	4.5	5	5.5	6	6.5	8	9	10	12.75

■□□□ BEGINNER	Projects for first-time knitters using basic knit and purl stitches. Minimal shaping.
■■□□ EASY	Projects using basic stitches, repetitive stitch patterns, simple color changes, and simple shaping and finishing.
■■■□ INTERMEDIATE	Projects with a variety of stitches, such as basic cables and lace, simple intarsia, double-pointed needles and knitting in the round needle techniques, mid-level shaping and finishing.
■■■■ EXPERIENCED	Projects using advanced techniques and stitches, such as short rows, fair isle, more intricate intarsia, cables, lace patterns, and numerous color changes.

GAUGE

Exact gauge is essential for proper fit. Needle size(s) given in instructions is/are merely a guide and should never be used without first making a sample swatch approximately 3-5" (7.5-12.5 cm) square in the stitch, yarn, and needle specified. Then measure the swatch, counting your stitches and rows or rounds carefully. If your swatch is larger or smaller than specified, make another, changing needle size to get the correct gauge. Keep trying until you find the size needle(s) that will give you the specified gauge.

SIZING

When choosing what size to make, you may want to measure a favorite top with similar styling and knit the size that has the nearest finished measurement. All of these garments are designed to be close-fitting with no ease other than what occurs naturally with knit fabrics. Finished chest measurement or finished body measurement is given depending on the style. In order to get a proper fit, measure under the bust for the body measurement and over the bust for chest measurement. Once you have chosen a size, you may adjust the body length to accommodate the actual measurements while adjusting the amount of yarn purchased accordingly.

KNITTING IN THE ROUND
USING CIRCULAR KNITTING NEEDLES

When you knit a tube, as for the body of a sweater, you are going to work around on the outside of the circle, with the right side of the knitting facing you. Using a circular knitting needle, cast on all stitches as instructed. Untwist and straighten the stitches on the needle to be sure that the cast on ridge lays on the inside of the needle and never rolls around the needle.
Hold the needle so that the ball of yarn is attached to the stitch closest to the **right** hand point. Place a marker on the right hand point to mark the beginning of the round.
To begin working in the round, knit the stitches on the left hand point **(Fig. 1)**.

Continue knitting around and around **without turning the work**; but for the first three rounds or so, check to be sure that the cast on edge has not twisted around the needle. If it has, it is impossible to untwist it. The only way to fix this is to rip it out and return to the cast on row.

Fig. 1

USING DOUBLE-POINTED KNITTING NEEDLES

When working a collar or sleeve that is too small to use a circular needle, double-pointed knitting needles are required. Divide the stitches into thirds and slip one-third of the stitches onto each of 3 double-pointed needles **(Fig. 2a)**, forming a triangle. Do **not** twist the cast on ridge. With the fourth needle, knit across the stitches on the first needle **(Fig. 2b)**. You will now have an empty needle with which to knit the stitches from the next needle. Work the first stitch of each needle firmly to prevent gaps. Continue working around without turning the work.

Fig. 2a

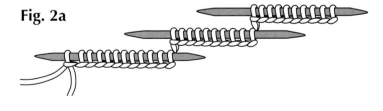

Fig. 2b

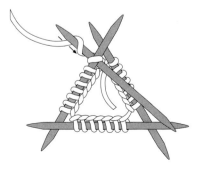

MARKERS

As a convenience to you, we have used markers to help distinguish the beginning of a round, a side, or the placement of a decrease. Place markers as instructed. You may use purchased markers or tie a length of contrasting color yarn around the needle. When you reach a marker on each round, slip it from the left needle to the right needle; remove it when it is no longer needed.

ZEROS

To consolidate the length of an involved pattern, zeros are sometimes used so that all sizes can be combined. For example, K 0{3-6-9} means that size X-Small would do nothing, size Small would K3, size Medium would K6, and size Large would K9.

DECREASES
KNIT 2 TOGETHER *(abbreviated K2 tog)*

Insert the **right** needle into the **front** of the first two stitches on the left needle as if to **knit** *(Fig. 3)*, then **knit** them together as if they were one stitch.

Fig. 3

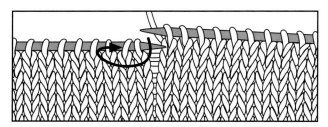

PURL 2 TOGETHER *(abbreviated P2 tog)*

Insert the **right** needle into the **front** of the first two stitches on the left needle as if to **purl** *(Fig. 4)*, then **purl** them together as if they were one stitch.

Fig. 4

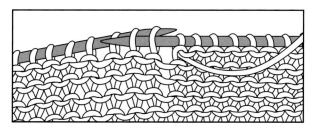

SLIP, SLIP, KNIT *(abbreviated SSK)*

With the yarn in back of work, separately slip two stitches as if to **knit** *(Fig. 5a)*. Insert the **left** needle into the **front** of both slipped stitches *(Fig. 5b)* and **knit** them together *(Fig. 5c)*.

Fig. 5a

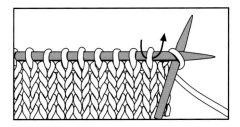

Fig. 5b

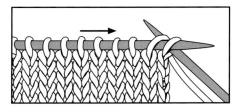

Fig. 5c

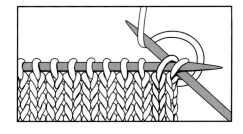

SLIP, SLIP, PURL *(abbreviated SSP)*

Separately slip two stitches as if to **knit**. Place these two stitches back onto the left needle. Insert the right needle into the **back** of both stitches from **back** to **front** *(Fig. 6)* and **purl** them together.

Fig. 6

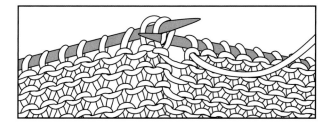

KNIT 3 TOGETHER *(abbreviated K3 tog)*

Insert the **right** needle into the **front** of the first three stitches on the left needle as if to **knit** *(Fig. 7)*, then **knit** them together as if they were one stitch.

Fig. 7

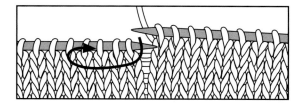

3-NEEDLE BIND OFF

Holding pieces with **right** side together and needles parallel to each other, insert a third needle as if to **knit** into the first stitch on the front needle **and** into the first stitch of the back needle *(Fig. 8)*. Knit these two stitches together and slip them off the needles. ★ Knit the next stitch on each needle together and slip them off the needles. To bind off, insert one left needle into the first stitch on the right needle and pull the first stitch over the second stitch and off the needle; repeat from ★ across until all of the stitches have been bound off.

Fig. 8

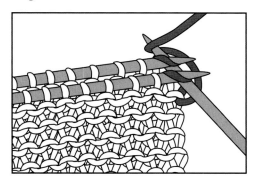

PICKING UP STITCHES

When instructed to pick up stitches, insert the needle from the **front** to the **back** under two strands at the edge of the worked piece *(Figs. 9a & b)*. Put the yarn around the needle as if to **knit**, then bring the needle with the yarn back through the stitch to the right side, resulting in a stitch on the needle.

Fig. 9a

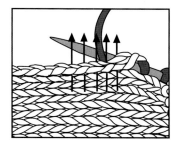

Fig. 9b

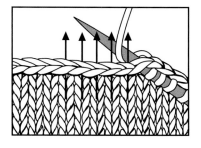

WEAVING SLEEVE SEAM

With the **right** side of both pieces facing you and edges even, sew through both pieces once to secure the seam. Insert the needle under the bar **between** the first and second stitches on the row and pull yarn through *(Fig. 10)*. Insert the needle under the next bar on the second side. Repeat from side to side, being careful to match rows. If the edges are different lengths, it may be necessary to insert the needle under two bars at one edge.

Fig. 10

CROCHET STITCHES
YARN OVER (abbreviated YO)
Bring the yarn **over** the top of the hook from **back** to **front**, catching the yarn with the hook and turning the hook slightly toward you to keep the yarn from slipping off (**Fig. 11**).

Fig. 11

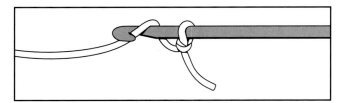

CHAIN (abbreviated ch)
YO, draw the yarn through the stitch on the hook (**Fig. 12**).

Fig. 12

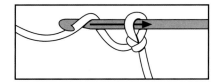

SLIP STITCH (abbreviated slip st)
Insert the hook in the stitch or space indicated, YO and draw through stitch or space and through loop on hook (**Fig. 13**).

Fig. 13

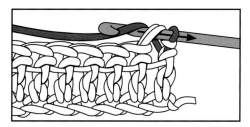

SINGLE CROCHET (abbreviated sc)
Insert the hook in the stitch or space indicated, YO and pull up a loop, YO and draw through both loops on hook (**Fig. 14**).

Fig. 14

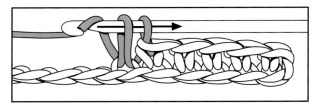

JOINING WITH SC
Begin with a slip knot on the hook. Insert the hook in the stitch or space indicated, YO and pull up a loop, YO and draw through both loops on hook (**Fig. 15**).

Fig. 15

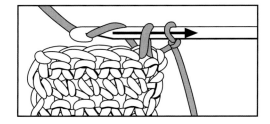

BACK LOOP ONLY
Work only in the loop(s) indicated by arrow (**Fig. 16**).

Fig. 16

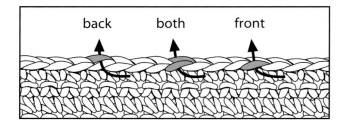

back   both   front

Yarn Information

Each item in this leaflet was made with Light, Medium, Bulky, or Super Bulky Weight yarn. Any brand of the same weight may be used. It is best to refer to the yardage/meters when determining how many balls or skeins to purchase. Remember, to arrive at the finished size, it is the GAUGE/TENSION that is important, not the brand of yarn.

For your convenience, listed below are the specific yarns used to create out photo models.

COLUMN DRESS
Lion® Cashmere Blend
#098 Cream

HALTER DRESS
Lion Brand® Wool-Ease® Chunky
#107 Bluebell

MOCK TURTLENECK
Lion Brand® Jiffy®
#111 Heather Blue

TURTLENECK SWEATER
Patons® Shetland Chunky Tweeds
#67128 Sea Ice

SHORT SLEEVE TOP
Lion Brand® Imagine
#099 Natural Cream

HALTER
Filatura Lanarota Luxor DK
Color number not available

SLEEVELESS TOP
Lion Brand® Jiffy®
#150 Pearl Grey

TUNIC
Plymouth Yarn Softer from Fibre Nobile & Lane Cervinia Collection
#3309 Orange

SPLIT NECK SHELL
Lion Brand® Jiffy®
#191 Violet

LONG SLEEVE SWEATER
Bernat® Softee® Chunky
Color number not available

TURTLENECK DRESS
Patons® Shetland Chunky
#03532 Deep Red

SKIRT
Sinfonia by Omega
Color number not available

V-NECK TOP
Lion Brand® Jiffy®
#173 Grass Green

SLEEVELESS TURTLENECK
Red Heart® Light & Lofty™
#9531 Plum

iCrochet

iEmbellish

iKnit

iQuilt

A NEW SERIES COMING IN 2007!

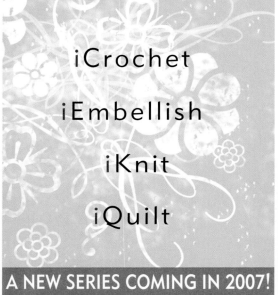